It'll Come
In Useful
One Day

It'll Come In Useful One Day

Intriguing Ways To Jog Your Memory

ROGER BRYAN

ILLUSTRATORS: Michael Heath, Ron McGeary,
Rachel Hardwick, Rhiannon Roberts,
Sophie Thomas, Hannah Bryan, Ela Bryan

PUBLISHED BY
LLANINA BOOKS

First published in Great Britain in 2010 by
Llanina Books
Plas Llanina
New Quay
Ceredigion SA45 9SJ

Third revised edition published in 2013

ISBN: 978-0-9567-199-2-8

Set in Times New Roman and Optima

This book can be ordered at:
www.rogerbryan.com

Printed and bound at Zrinski DD, Croatia.

Contents

Illustrations

Michael Heath: cover, pp 2, 8
Ron McGeary: pp 22, 73, 129
Rachel Hardwick: pp 31, 176, 218
Rhiannon Roberts: pp 135, 154, 185
Sophie Thomas: pp 37, 77
Ela Bryan: pp 36, 67, 68, 71, 149, 172, 233
Roger Sims: Graphics pp 44, 109, 222, 223
Hannah Bryan: pp 54, 145, 206, 217
Hannah Bryan and Billie Christopher: p 57

www.rogerbryan.com
www.llaninabooks.com
www.ronmcgeary.co.uk
www.rachelhardwick.com
www.rhiannonart.co.uk

Foreword

IT'LL Come In Useful One Day was one of my late mother's favourite sayings along with 'You'll catch your death of cold' and 'There's plenty of room for growth'. This book is full of ideas which, I hope, will indeed 'Come in useful one day'.

It is a personal collection of mnemonics, acronyms, verses, old wives' tales, rhymes, word play and puns, acrostics, images plus a smattering of old jokes, all designed to help you retain and then remember and recall bits of information.

Many were collected over a period of more than 30 years working as a journalist, and others I have created myself. Each entry is aimed at being useful in some situation or other: a school or university exam, an interview, an application for a job, at a dinner party, a school or pub quiz, an appearance on Pointless or even Who Wants To Be A Millionaire? Indeed, as we shall see, it may even help you to keep your job.

This third edition was born out of the success of the first two editions. I hope that in all possible ways you will find it a book to remember.

CHAPTER 1

Introduction

Mnemonics: *n pl.* (usu. treated as *sing*).
1 the art of assisting and improving
memory, especially by artificial aids
(but not performance-enhancing drugs);
2 a system of precepts intended to aid
and improve the memory.
[med L. *mnemonics,* f. Gk *mnemonikos*]

From Mnemosyne, daughter of Gaia (Earth) and Uranus
(Heaven), whom the Greeks so revered that they made
her the goddess of memory. She was the most beautiful
of all the goddesses, attracting Zeus himself; their
progeny were the Nine Muses, the goddesses of all
things creative.

Even mnemonics needs a mnemonic to remember how to spell it. It's one of a very few words in the English language to start with the letters mn, but that may not be enough of a reminder. Here's one:

Mnemonics Neatly Eliminate Man's Only Nemesis: Insufficient Cerebral Storage

Not a good start. It's certainly useful to have a mnemonic mnemonic, but this is not it – you have to know how to spell the word in the first place to get going.

So how about this?

My Nice Editor Measures Out News In Columns

It's shorter, it works and it might just give you a leg-up sometime in the publishing world.

Mnemonics are reasonably well known to people of a certain age, but they fell out of fashion in the 1970s and 80s.

The late Poet Laureate Ted Hughes blamed it all on the Puritan/Protestant ascendancy in the English Civil War 1642-48 (which is going back a bit, to be honest) and the attempt then to banish imagery from all aspects of life.

> 'The same spirit also banished from the schools the old-established memory techniques that used imagery, and replaced it with learning by rote. The discarded methods were soon forgotten…If any attempt was made to reintroduce them, they were dismissed as tricks and cheating.'

A Publisher's Note in A Dictionary of Mnemonics (1972) demonstrated the gravity of the situation: 'Times are bad for the memory aid. Mnemonics were used in Ancient Greece, but today their enemies say that learning from them is like learning about sex from dirty jokes.'

But mnemonics seem to have made something of a comeback recently. So let's come to the aid of the memory aid, with the help of a few (clean) jokes perhaps along the way. Let's hear it for the mnemonic.

Perhaps the most famous mnemonic, and certainly one of the best remembered, is the one for the colours of the rainbow…

Richard of York Gave Battle In Vain

Red, Orange, Yellow, Green, Blue, Indigo, Violet

Millions of children in the UK down the ages have learned the colours of the visible spectrum – the colours of the rainbow – from this, and strangely enough it appears to be quite popular in the US as well. To me, it has always seemed a very dull, almost meaningless mnemonic, albeit an effective one.

So who was Richard of York, and where and in what circumstances did he give battle in vain? One theory is that it was Richard III, who was defeated in 1485 by Henry Tudor at the Battle of Bosworth Field. This was a major battle that established the Tudor dynasty and ended The War of the Roses. Richard was the Duke of Gloucester, although a member of the House of York.

It seems just as likely that our Richard of York was none other than the Grand Old Duke of York, the one with 10,000 men. Richard Plantagenet, 3rd Duke of York, was the father of Richard III, and he himself had been defeated and killed in The War of the Roses at the Battle of Wakefield in 1460.

The castle was on top of an old Norman motte and bailey fortress, and after marching his men to the top, where he was impregnable, the Duke was informed that another large column of men was about to relieve him. So he decided to go to engage the enemy, and marched his men back down the hill to join combat against the Lancastrians, only for the Duke and his troops to meet a hasty and nasty end.

So our Richard of York left a grand old legacy . . . a nursery rhyme known by millions:

The Grand Old Duke of York

He had ten thousand men

He marched them up to the top of the hill

And he marched them down again.

When they were up, they were up.

And when they were down, they were down.

And when they were only halfway up

They were neither up nor down.

. . . and one of the most famous mnemonics ever.

Although Richard of York is used in the US, the default American mnemonic is:

Roy G. Biv

It's a strange name and Mr RG Biv (or it could be Mr RG B the Fourth) hasn't got any of the historical and royal pedigree of our Grand Old Duke, but, well, it works. Even if Biv does mean sewer pipe in Hebrew!

After the Second World War, this one was in circulation in the UK:

Remember O Ye Germans, Britain Is Victorious

And in the 1950s, pupils at a girls' school in York were able to boast:

Rowntrees of York
Give Best In Value

Unfortunately, the chocolate and sweet company Rowntrees was later taken over by Nestlé.

My favourite was told to me by an Australian sub-editor doing some shifts in Fleet Street:

Rip Out Your Guts Before I Vomit

It's concise and has a graphic Australian directness to it, and I'm sure that it will be met with appreciation and approval by today's teenagers. Certainly, my teenage son swears by it.

I considered this as the title of the book, but friends with more discernment and infinitely better taste advised against it.

THE SIEGE OF SIDNEY STREET

CHAPTER 2

Word Pairs

Siege/Seize:

The **Si**ege of **Si**dney Street   (**Si Si**)

Once you know this mnemonic, you will never misspell siege (or seize) ever again, guaranteed. (This is a non-binding contractual promise on the part of the author). You may not think that this is of much importance, but on a day off when I worked at the London Evening Standard, I was walking down Oxford Street in central London and was mortified to see the banner front page headline on the news-stand with the word

in 108pt type. This is this big. And this WRONG.

My first reaction was 'Oh No' and the second was 'Well, glad I'm on a day off'. It was part of my job to write these headlines, and it doesn't pay to misspell siege (or any other word come to that) in block capitals that are one-and-a-half inches high and read by more than a million people.

I learned this mnemonic back in the 70s, and it has stuck with me ever since. I was told it when I worked on The Yorkshire Post by an old and haggard chain-smoking news sub-editor who had seen better days. (He may possibly have been at the incident himself!) I have never spelled Siege incorrectly since then and never heard or seen the mnemonic anywhere else.

So back to The Siege of Sidney Street. For the benefit of younger readers – in this instance, anybody under 90 – this was an incident that took place in the East End of London in 1911. A robbery went wrong and the villains, East European anarchists, fled and ended up in a house in Sidney Street.

The police surrounded the house, which subsequently caught fire, and the then Home Secretary, a young Winston Churchill, forbade the Fire Brigade from putting it out. Churchill was later criticised for his intervention, which was widely seen as a publicity exercise.

And for the person who wants to know too much: Alfred Hitchcock used the siege as the climax of his film The Man Who Knew Too Much in 1934.

An ex-colleague, the late Jim Anderson, former splash

sub-editor at the London Evening News, the Evening Standard's arch rival at the time, relates the story of how one day a reader rang in to point out that Siege had been misspelled in a headline. The editor went ballistic and ordered that the word SIEGE be typeset in letters three-foot high and hung over the sub-editors'desk. In those days, it could easily have been a sub-editor that was hung. Siege was never misspelled after that.

On reflection, we came to the conclusion that every newspaper in the land, and most probably the English-speaking world, must have misspelled Siege in a headline at one time or another. So remember the Siege of Sidney Street.

The mnemonic also applies to seize . Now you know how to spell siege, you know how to spell seize – it's just the opposite of siege.

SEize the day, sail the high SEas.

Practise/Practice License/Licence

S is the verb, and **C** is the noun
That's the rule that runs the town.

The doctor practises at his Harley Street practice.
The local pub is fully licensed – it has a licence to sell alcohol.

In the US, confusingly, it is the other way round.

Complement/Compliment

Regularly mixed up, especially for some reason on the flyers you get through your door from local takeaways, restaurants, minicab firms etc. There's generally a complementary half bottle of wine in there somewhere. And also, unforgivably, on menus: the Australian Cabernet Sauvignon 2007 perfectly compliments the medium-rare kangaroo burger in a koala jus with a julienne of eucalyptus leaves. If only wine bottles could talk.

It's easy – a COMPLEment COMPLEtes.
A compliment doesn't – it is something else entirely: an expression of courteous praise.

So a full complement is just that – the complete number of sailors to man a ship for example.
And a bottle of Chateau Margaux (any year) would certainly complement any meal.

A full compliment would be something completely different – fulsome praise in fact.

Complementary medicine completes the medical circle. This is correct.

Complimentary medicine is something completely different. Instead of saying 'Morning, you look rough today', the doctor greets you with: 'You're looking especially healthy today. Oh, and I like your jumper too.'

Complimentaries have a separate meaning as freebies.

Stationary/Stationery

StationAry – imagine that you are on A train in A station, not moving, not going anywhere, you know the sort of thing. You are stationAry.

StatioNEry – think of Notepaper and Envelopes. You are in a statioNEry shop, thinking of buying Notepaper and Envelopes. You are about to purchase some statioNEry.

Here's a strange thing: have you noticed that on the concourse at all big railway stations there is a stationery shop?

Principal/Principle

Principal:
As a noun, treat the princiPAL as your chief PAL.
As an adjective, treat him as the leading boy.

Principle:
None of the above. As a rule, treat it as a fundamental truth or the basis of a moral code.

Your chief friend may be a high principal at the college. He may, or may not, be a man of high principle, although we will assume he is.

Effect/Affect

This is a complicated one, because the two words serve both as verbs and nouns.

To effect means to bring about, to accomplish:
The win was effected by a late penalty goal.

To affect means to have some influence on something:
The penalty decision directly affected the outcome of the game.

The effect means the result or consequence of something:
The effect of the result was that the Rovers stayed top of the table.

The affect is used in psychiatry, quite rare, meaning a mental state or emotion: not to be confused with the effect that watching your football team has on your mental state.

None of this is mnemonic, but you will often see this:

RAVEN
Remember: Affect Verb, Effect Noun

This is wrong, because we know that the two words are both verbs and nouns, but it is as well to know their different meanings.

Stalagmites/Stalactites

An easy one this:

Mites crawl up and Tites fall down.

This is an old fourth-form classic and is still the best for remembering whether stalagmites or stalactites go up from the floor or hang down from above.

Desert/Dessert

One Sugar or two:
One in the desert,
Twice as much for that sweet dessert.

There/Their/They're

Directions for There:
Is it HERE or is it tHERE?

Ownership for Their:
HEIRs inherit tHEIR fortunes.

They're is a contraction, a shortening of They are.

They're on their way there

Ensure/Insure

Ensure is to make certain that something happens.
Insure is to buy a policy to protect you from loss, or theft.

An insurance policy was taken out to protect the finances
of the village fete in the event of inclement weather: this
ensured that the event would not make a loss.

Hypothermia/Hyperthermia

It's important to get this right if you are in the medical
profession, not that you wouldn't of course.

Hypo generally means under or below normal.
Hypothermia: an abnormally low body temperature.

Hyper generally means over or above normal
and has gained a meaning of excessive. Hyper hyper.
Hyperactive: excessively active, an adjective generally
describing a child.

Coruscating/Excoriating

Quite regularly mixed up in the quality newspapers
(the popular newspapers never using the words).
Coruscating means brilliant, shining, sparkly (from the
Latin coruscare = to glitter)
Excoriate means remove part of the skin of a person;
strip or peel off skin; censure severely (from the Latin
corium = hide).
Not the same thing at all.

Fewer/Less

This is an important one, as these words are quite often used incorrectly in the newspapers and on television. My mnemonic here is neat and concise. Ignore the fact that it is illogical.

Fewer sewers, less mess

Fewer for numbers, less for mass/amount

Quite often wrong at supermarket check-out queues: Less than Five Items is wrong; it should be Fewer than Five Items.

If you can put a number in front of the noun or pronoun, or the noun/pronoun is a plural, use fewer.
If you can't put a number before the noun or pronoun use less.
Eg: seven people, six people, fewer people
Eg: seven sewers, six sewers, fewer sewers

We had fewer cricket matches last summer because of the bad weather.

Less cricket was played last summer because of the bad weather.

The banks had less bad debt than last year.
My son had fewer debts than last year.

(The sentence is correct: would that it was also true!)

Due to/Owing to

This is a bit of a technical one and many reference books don't mention it at all. Even über-pedant Kingsley Amis could find no reason for any distinction in The King's English. 'I have investigated the origins of this rule, and nothing substantial or satisfactory emerges. It seems to be just a rule'.

But there is a difference. Due to should be used as an adjective. (It must therefore describe a noun). Owing to is a preposition.

Due to tends to mean *caused by*
Owing to tends to mean *because of*

a) The match was cancelled due to bad weather. This is not correct. Due to bad weather is an adjective, describing the noun match. The match was not due to the bad weather, the cancellation was.

b) The match was cancelled owing to bad weather. This is OK.   *(owing to = because of).*

c) The cancellation of the match was due to bad weather. This is correct. The cancellation *was* due to bad weather.   *(due to = caused by).*

d) The cancellation of the match was owing to bad weather. Correct.   *(owing to = because of).*

e) Due to bad weather, the match had to be cancelled
This is not correct, and it doesn't sound right either.

f) Owing to bad weather, the match was cancelled.
Correct.   *(owing to = because of).*

In practice, the general rules are

Treat *Due to* as an adjective
Treat *Owing to* as a preposition.

A general rule which should help to keep you out of trouble is:

Never start a sentence with Due to.

Passed/Past

These words can be extremely confusing:
Messi ran past the defender and then passed the ball.

> *Passed* is the past tense and the past participle of the verb to pass.
> The soldiers passed in front of the Cenotaph.
>
> *Past* acts mainly as a preposition, but also acts as an adjective.
> The soldiers marched past the Cenotaph. *(preposition)*
> First past the post. *(preposition)*
> Times past. *(adjective)*

Its/It's

This is not a mnemonic, so maybe this should not be here – but it's an important, and short, entry.

Its
means something belongs to someone or something, a possessive.

It's
is a diminution, a contraction of it is or it has.

Grimethorpe was proud of its mine.
(The pit was in the South Yorkshire town, which was proud both of its mine and its famous brass band, which also belonged to the town).

Before the coal industry was nationalised in 1947, the colliery owner was able to sing: It's mine, it's mine, it's all mine.

Whose/Who's

Whose is a possessive pronoun.

Who's is a diminution again, a shortening of who is or who has.

Whose Life is it Anyway?
Who's Been Sleeping in my Bed?
Who's Who.

Your/You're

Same again:

Your is a possessive pronoun.

You're is a contraction, a shortening of you are.

> Your place or mine?
> You're fired!
> You're welcome

That brings us to the Aberrant Apostrophe.

The Greengrocer's Apostrophe

Generally applied wrongly and needlessly. It denotes a process in which greengrocers, especially those with market stalls, fill up the pepper pot with apostrophes every morning and liberally sprinkle the contents over all their signs. So we get:

APPLE'S, ORANGE'S, BANANA'S, and POTATO'S, POTATOE'S, POTATOS' and POTATOES' where the words are simple plurals and do not need any punctuation. Co's lettuce was a favourite of mine.

This incorrect use of the apostrophe was a particular irritant to the master of writing style Keith Waterhouse, who founded the Association for the Abolition of the Aberrant Apostrophe more than 20 years ago in the Daily Mail.

He wrote: 'In the AAAA's Black Apostrophe Museum, which you are welcome to visit, you will find an advertisement from The Guardian for Technical Author's; a circular from the National Council for the Training of Journalists, if you please, containing the phrase "as some editor's will know"; and an announcement from Austin Rover about the new Maestro's'.

Lynne Truss willingly picked up the baton in her excellent bestseller Eats, Shoots & Leaves in 2003.

'No matter that you have a Ph.D and have read all Henry James twice. If you still persist in writing, "Good food at it's best," you deserve to be struck by lightning, hacked up on the spot and buried in an unmarked grave.'

A bit radical you might say, but in a chapter on apostrophes, she identifies a long list of categories of misuse:

Pupil's entrance   *(a very selective school)*.

Giant Kid's Playground   *(empty – everyone is terrified of the Big Kid)*.

Cyclist's only   *(what?)*

Childrens education   *(in a letter from the head of education at the National Union of Teachers)*.

The full name and title of person who's details are given in Section 02   *(on UK passport application form)*.

Gateaux's   *(just wonderful)*.

I once noticed at my local municipal sports ground that the bowls were separated into two boxes: Bowls and Jack's, and my local wet fish shop generally has Tub's of Prawns on offer. One of the attractions at our local football club fete this year was Donkey's.

Recent developments do not bode well for the poor apostrophe. In 2009, Birmingham City Council unilaterally scrapped apostrophes from council signs for the sake of 'simplicity'. So St Paul's Square (the Square of St Paul) is now St Pauls Square. (They must have discovered the existence of more than one St Paul).

And Waterstone's caused a bit of a stir in 2012 when they dropped the apostrophe from their name. It was pointed out, to no avail, that this might prove a mistake for a bookseller trying to attract literate customers.

In this instance the company did have a point as the eponymous Waterstone had had nothing to do with the book chain since 1993 and the company was sold to a Russian billionaire in 2010.

Sainsbury's have been producing an A5 flyer featuring both Sainsbury's and Sainsburys in display type about 30 point high, on the same page, which is confusing to say the least.

I am indebted to a correspondent to The Guardian for reporting seeing a teenage girl with a tattoo on her back from shoulder to shoulder in letters two inches high – NO REGRET's.

Not yet...

CHAPTER 3

50 Hard Words

Spelling is an increasing problem in Britain. In one survey recently, six out of ten 15-year-olds could not write ten lines without making at least one spelling mistake. And it is not just young people: adults can struggle, too. Here are 50 difficult-to-spell words with ways of remembering them.

Separate was judged to be the most misspelled word in a survey in 2010. Most mnemonics for the word Separate are poor and I hope my example in this chapter is an improvement.

In his excellent book Every Good Boy Deserves Fudge, Rod L Evans has a section on spelling that contains around 1,000 words. But nobody is going to learn the mnemonics for that number of words. In this instance, less is more.

You can even buy spelling dictionaries (think about it). If you find spelling difficult, my advice would be to buy a small dictionary that you will find easier to navigate around and just look up any word with which you are struggling . For reference, using my Concise

Oxford Dictionary, the middle page is M, Magyar in fact. The first quarter almost reaches E (dress) and the third quarter starts at S (sarong). So if you open the dictionary about halfway, you will be around letter M, and if you open it three-quarters through, you will probably be on letter S.

It is as well to know how to spell. The Spellcheck on your home (or work) computer is not the answer. A long time ago somebody on the City Desk used Spellcheck on an article about merchant bankers Morgan Grenfell, all references to which ended up on the page, but mercifully not in the paper, as Morning Greenfly.

The inadequacies of the computer Spellchecker (and the illogicality and perversity of spelling in English) are highlighted by The English Spelling Society, and if you are interested, its website is worth visiting. Here is a poem that shows that the one thing you can't count on is – Spellcheck. The whole poem has 12 verses; four are published here.

So. . . along the lines of the acronym created by Kelly Johnson, chief engineer at Lockheed aviation:

KISS
Keep It Simple, Stupid

How about?

DROSS
Don't Rely On Spellcheck, Stupid

Candidate for
a Pullet Surprise

By Margo Roark

I have a spelling checker,
It came with my PC.
It plane lee marks four my revue
Miss steaks aye can knot sea.

Eye strike a key and a type a word
And weight for it to say
Weather eye am wrong oar rite
It shows me straight away.

As soon as a mist ache is made
It nose bee fore two long
And eye can put the error rite
It's rarely ever wrong.

Eye have run this poem threw it
Eye am shore your pleased two no
It's letter perfect awl the weigh
My checker tolled me sew.

I ran the poem through my Word Spellcheck and it came up with the following three suggestions:

Second verse: Weather eye am – suggests is!
Last verse: Eye have run – suggests has!
              It's letter perfect – suggests a hyphen.
I rest my case

This is not a mnemonic, but nonetheless a very important piece of advice that definitely will come in useful:

> Always But Always
> Check Your Written
> Work, Twice.
> And Then Again . . .

whether it be a letter or an article or an exam paper or anything else. Not checking your work, or least not checking it properly, can have huge consequences.

Read this cautionary tale from times gone by. Robert Barker and Martin Lucas were the Royal Printers in London in the early part of the 17th century, and publishers of the Bible in 1631 that was to be a reprint of the 1611 King James Authorised Version of the Bible. They must have wished they had checked their work properly because the Bible became known as the Wicked Bible, or the Sinners' Bible.

The reason was that in Exodus 20:14, a three-letter word was omitted by the compositors. Unfortunately the missing word was 'not' – and even more unfortunately for the printers, it was in the section on the Ten Commandments. The Seventh Commandment now read as an exhortation: 'Thou shalt commit adultery.' Go forth and . . .

The mistake enraged Charles I, who ordered the printers to the Star Chamber, where they were deprived of their printers' licence, which put them out of business. All the 1,000 Bibles were withdrawn from circulation and burned, although a very small number survived.

More recently, Jonathan Franzen, heralded as the new Great American Novelist, encountered a similar problem in 2010 when the British publication of his much-awaited second novel Freedom had to be withdrawn after the printers used an earlier, uncorrected version of the text rather than the final draft. The author spotted hundreds of mistakes in spelling, grammar and characterisation. More than 8,000 books had been sold, and 80,000 printed, which were then hastily withdrawn.

It can't have done anything for Mr Franzen's humour that his excellent and much-acclaimed first novel was called The Corrections.

Always check your work (cont). This bilingual sign in Swansea, South Wales, looked fine until it was pointed out that the Welsh translated as: I am not in the office at the moment. Send any work to be translated.

The council's highways department had sent off the English to be translated (probably at lunchtime) and the reply came back as an automated email message in Welsh. Oops.

Always check your work, doubly so if you are working in a foreign language.

Acceptable
I will accept any table

Accident
Dent after two cars collide

Accessible
I am always accessIble, I am

Accommodation
ACCoMModation:
Comfy Chairs Only, Many Mod-cons

Aero plane
All Engines Running OK

All right
Alright is alwrong

Apparent
Clearly, A Pushy Parent

Argument
Don't argue – there's no e

Arithmetic
A Rat In The House
Might Eat The Ice Cream

Assassin
The SS strike twice

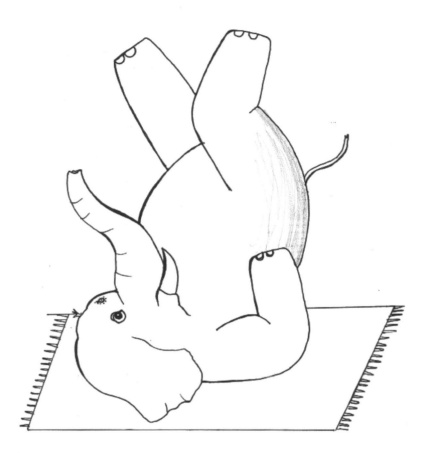

Beauty
Big Elephants Are Usually Trying Yoga

Because
Betty Eats Cheese And Usually Some Eggs. From my younger daughter, who says she finds it very useful.

Believe
Don't beLIEve a LIE

Benefit
Ben E. Fit   (Ben E. King's long lost brother)

Broccoli
C.Coli   (E.Coli's long lost brother)

Cemetery
Three eees. You are walking though a cemetery at night and something jumps out and screams Eeehhh – three ees.

Committee
Doubles all round: double M, double T and double E

ConSCious
Conscious and Self-Conscious

Consensus
By general agreement, think consent. Nothing to do with the census.

Definite
If it's finite, then there is a good chance that it's definite.

Desiccate:
Sic Cate has a dry sense of humour

Desperate
Nil DesPERandum
Think PERil

Diarrhoea
Dash In A Real Rush Home – Or Else Accident!

Difficulty
Mrs D, Mrs I, Mrs FFI; Mrs C, Mrs U, Mrs LTY
– Courtesy of Roald Dahl in Matilda.

Disappoint
Di's a People's Princess

Ecstasy
No X please, we're ecstatic

Embarrass
Emba went **R**eally **R**ed **A**nd **S**miled **S**hyly

Exceed
Don't exc-eed the sp-eed limit

Friend
Always a FriEND in the END

Gauge
Get A Useful General Estimate

Geography
General Eisenhower's Old Girl Rode
A Pony Home Yesterday

Graffito (pl graffiti)
Two fingers, one toe (keep moving)
Graffiti: Still two fingers, one tea (keep moving)

Grammar
A ram in the mirror – ram/mar

Haemorrhage
Help! An Emergency Most Often Requiring Rapid
Hospital Attention

Harass
Hit and run donkey

Hypocrisy
Think hypocrite

Indispensable
Only the most Able people are indispensAble (or so
they tell us)

Inoculate
Usually by in-jection

Irresistible
I'm IrresIstIble (yes you are)

Liaison
Lia is on
(for a secret meeting tonight – it's dangerous).

Mediterranean
Terra firma
The sea in the middle of the land, the
Medi-TERRA-nean being a landlocked sea.

Misspell
Think of that nice English teacher Miss Pell.

Minuscule
Sounds like i, but it's a u. Think of minus.
Originally meaning a small cursive script, it has now
taken on the meaning of tiny.

In a survey of spelling on internet newsgroup sites,
minuscule was the word most often spelled incorrectly
– 68% of the time. And often in newspapers.

It comes from the Latin minusculus meaning rather
less.

Necessary
One collar, two sleeves needed

Noticeable
You are able to see the notice

para**l l** e**l l**ines

Parallel
Parallel lines; four ls

Privilege
Privilege can be judged to be **vile**

Psycho
Please Send Your Cards Home Often

(So we can keep track of where you are, you nutcase.)

I just can't read Psychotherapist as anything other than Psycho The Rapist. Perhaps I need treatment? So will you now.

And watch out for his long-lost brother Hypno, who is a very dangerous sort.

Queue
QUeen **E**lizabeth **U**nderstands **E**verything

Rhythm:
Reggae Has Your Two Hips Moving

SePARate
Pull them aPARt
Keep them aPARt
SePARate them, Mum

In a recent survey, this was the word misspelled the most. This mnemonic here should do the job. The standard mnemonic for remembering how to spell Separate is: Remember it contains a rat. It doesn't work for me.

Vacuum
V double U, nice cars to clean

i before e, except after c

This is a pretty general rule only.

There is an addendum to this:

Or when sounded a
as in neighbour and weigh
And weird is just weird.

This is a well-known mnemonic, owing its popularity to its brevity as much as anything, and indeed is the title of a recent book on the subject of mnemonics. In practice, there are more than 100 exceptions to the rule, among them:

> Neither, either, forfeit, eight, height, protein, seize, science, ancient, efficient, beige, reign, foreign, weight, caffeine, freight, leisure, reindeer, sovereign, et al…

It has been calculated (by whom, I know not) that the i before e rule applies to only 11 out of the 10,000 most common words in English.

There was even a mnemonic for some of the exceptions:

> Sheila, the counterfeiter, was seized by
> a weird thought at the weir.

In fact, the Department of Education has sent out advice to teachers as part of the National Primary Strategy that the i before e except after c rule is no longer worth teaching because of the number of exceptions.

The ten most common words in most languages make up 25% of everything we say, so if you're learning a foreign language, it's probably a good idea to learn them, if you don't know them already: the, be (am, is, are), to, if, and, a(n), in, that, have (has, had), I (me). In most languages, half of all conversation is made up of 100 words.

Plurals of words ending in o
(A general rule of thumb)

For a word ending in o preceded by a vowel,
add S

For a word ending in o preceded by a consonant,
add ES.

For a word relating to music and ending in o,
add S

Eg: video, videos; radio, radios; stereo, stereos.
potato, potatoes; tomato, tomatoes.
piano, pianos; solo, solos; piccolo, piccolos.

Ghoti

This was the word that George Bernard Shaw famously created to illustrate the problems presented by English spelling and pronunciation (see also next page). The word ghoti is, of course, pronounced fish:

gh as in enough, o as in women and ti as in nation.

When I started to learn Welsh a couple of years ago, I complained to my (Welsh) brother-in-law about how difficult it was. He then emailed me this poem, saying I was lucky I did not have to learn English as a foreign language. I think he had a point.

I take it you already know,
Of *tough* and *bough* and *cough* and *dough*?
Others may stumble, but not you,
On *hiccough*, *thorough*, *lough* and *through*.
Well done. And now you wish, perhaps,
To learn of less familiar traps.
Beware of *heard*, a dreadful *word*,
That looks like *beard* and sounds like *bird*.
And *dead*: it's *said* like *bed*, not *bead*,
For goodness' sake, don't call it *deed*.
Watch out for *meat* and *great* and *threat*,
They rhyme with *suite* and *straight* and *debt*.
A *moth* is not a *moth* in *mother*,
Nor *both* in *bother*, *broth* in *brother*.
And *here* is not a match for *there*
Nor *dear* and *fear* for *bear* and *pear*.
And then there's *dose* and *rose* and *lose* –
Just look them up – and *goose* and *choose*.
And *cork* and *work*, and *card* and *ward*,
And *font* and *front*, and *word* and *sword*.
And *do* and *go*, and *thwart* and *cart*.
Come, come, I've hardly made a start.
A dreadful language! Man Alive!
I'd mastered it when I was five.

CHAPTER 4

Numbers

This is the dumbest mnemonic in the book, so here it is at the start of this chapter to get it out of the way. It is a mnemonic for the first ten integers:

Only The Truly Forgetful Fellow Should Summon Each Number Thusly

Someone somewhere spent a fair amount of time thinking up that one. Sorry, ignore the mnemonic and just remember

1, 2, 3, 4, 5, 6, 7, 8, 9, 10

If you need a mnemonic to remember these numbers, you are reading the wrong book. In fact, I'm surprised you got this far.

Square roots

The number of letters in each word represents a digit.

I wish I knew – the root of two

1.414

O procure for me – the root of three

1.732

So we can arrive – at the root of five

2.236

We need more logistics –

for the square root of six

2.449

It rhymes with heaven – the root of seven

2.646

The Pythagoras Theorem

For finding the length of the sides of a right-angled triangle

$$a^2 + b^2 = c^2$$

Where a and b are the short sides of the triangle, and c is the hypotenuse (longest side).

> *The square on the hypotenuse is equal to the sum of the squares on the other two sides.*

The mnemonic for this is an old school favourite. I can't remember many laughs in maths lessons when I was at school; in fact, this was probably the only one. Here goes:

A Red Indian chief (you can tell how old the story is) had three squaws, all of whom were about to give birth. He laid one squaw on a bear hide; the second squaw on a lion hide; and the third he laid out on a hippopotamus hide.

When they went into labour, the mother on the bear hide gave birth to a son. Soon after, the mother on the lion hide also gave birth to a son. Finally the squaw laid out on the hippopotamus hide gave birth to twin boys. So…

> *The sons of the squaw on the hippopotamus are equal to the sons of the squaws on the other two hides.*

The Metric system:

King Hector Doesn't
Usually Drink Cold Milk

Kids Hate Doing Maths
During Cloudy Mondays

Kilo, Hecto, Deca, (Unit/Metre), Deci, Centi, Milli.

NUMBERS / prefixes & factors

PETA	10^{15}	**1,000,000,000,000,000**
TERA	10^{12}	**1,000,000,000,000**
GIGA	10^{9}	**1,000,000,000**
MEGA	10^{6}	**1,000,000**
KILO	10^{3}	**1,000**
HECTO	10^{2}	**100**
DECA	10^{1}	**10**
	10^{0}	**1**
DECI	10^{-1}	**0.1**
CENTI	10^{-2}	**0.01**
MILLI	10^{-3}	**0.001**
MICRO	10^{-6}	**0.000,001**
NANO	10^{-9}	**0.000,000,001**
PICO	10^{-12}	**0.000,000,000,001**
FEMTO	10^{-15}	**0.000,000,000,000,001**

Here is a mnemonic for bigger numbers – they do have an everyday relevance in the computer age:

Killer Megan
Googles Terror Pet

Kilo, Mega, Giga, Tera, Peta.

1 Kilobyte = 1,000 bytes

1 Megabyte = 1,000 Kilobytes

1 Gigabyte = 1,000 Megabytes

1 Terabyte = 1,000 Gigabytes

1 Petabyte = 1,000 Terabytes = 1,000,000 Gigabytes

It wasn't too long ago that hard drive space was described in megabytes. Gigabyte is the common term today, and some new computers already have 1, 1.5 or even 2 terabyte hard drives. The next level up is:

Exabyte, Zettabyte, Yottabyte, Brontobyte

It might be some time before we see these terms. It would take approximately 11 trillion years to download a Yottabyte file from the internet using super speed broadband. It can be compared to the world wide web in that the entire internet takes up about a yottabyte, which is 10^{24}. Should be called lottabytes.

At the other end of the table, one byte is eight connected bits (b-inary dig-its) – ie eight 1s or 0s side by side. It can store 2^8 values, which is 256. And 4 bits, the equivalent of half a byte, is a nibble. Boom, boom!

Roman numerals

Lucy Can't Drink Milk

L =   50
C =   100
D =   500
M =1,000

Intra-Venous X-ray

I = 1
V = 5
X = 10

When left is small and right is bigger
Subtract the left from the right-hand figure.

eg IV (1 subtracted from 5) = 4
    IX (1 subtracted from 10) = 9

MCMLIX = 1000 + [1000 − 100] + 50 + [10 − 1].
1959 – a good year, my wife was born.

What number do you get by adding up all the Roman
numerals in order? M D C L X V I = 1666, the year of
the Great Fire of London. I include this only because I
have been told it is a popular pub quiz question.

Roman numerals have had their day, but they still survive – sometimes in the most unexpected places. Gravestones and inscriptions on monuments are obvious places; also to number the pages at the front of books, as they do here; also monarchs take Roman numerals: Henry VIII, not Henry 8th, or Henry the 1/8. Popes take them too. The number of players in a sporting team is often expressed in Roman numerals: school football and hockey teams are the First XI and Second XI and the First XV for rugby union.

Another place where Roman numerals survive is on clocks and watches. Interestingly, number 4 is often represented by IIII instead of IV. There have been a number of theories for this, but the best one seems to be one of aesthetics – it looks better because it complements and balances the number VIII on the opposite side of the clockface. Another theory was that by using IIII, there would be 28 numbers around the clockface – four Xs, four Vs and 20 Is. This would have been helpful at the casting stage because the smiths could get away with making four moulds for the 28 numbers: each mould containing one X, one V and five Is that could then be separated and re-arranged into the correct order.

The unexpected places where they live on is in America – the film industry, for instance, often puts the date the film was released at the end in roman numerals. Film sequels also take roman numerals: Rocky II, III, IV, V, Balboa, VII; Superman II, III, IV. This gave rise to an apocryphal story of an American film producer, who having seen Henry V, asked what the first four films in the series were like.

The annual American outpouring of hyperbole – Superbowl, the final of the American Football season – takes Roman numerals. The 2012 event played in Indianapolis was Superbowl XLVI [50 -10] = 40 + 6 = 46. And an event called WrestleMania, an annual American wrestle-fest, also uses Roman numerals – the event in Miami 2012 being XXVIII.

The XXX Olympic Games in London in 2012 were the 30th of modern times that started in Athens in 1896. At least the Olympics can claim some classical connections.

Map-reading

Read the horizontal X co-ordinates first, and then the vertical Y grid.

Eg: a map-reading of 123456,
read 123 along the bottom and then 456 up the side.

Onwards and upwards

Come in the door before going upstairs.
— Army recruit instruction on how to give map references.

Sines and Cosines

These trigonometric functions are used to relate the angles of a triangle to the length of its sides.

Sine = Opposite/Hypotonuse
Cosine = Adjacent/Hypotonuse
Tangent = Opposite/Adjacent

SOH-CAH-TOA (sounds like Krakatoa)

Sailors Often Have   Silly Old Harry
Curly Auburn Hair   Caught A Herring
Till Old Age   Trawling Off Aberdeen

Smiles of Happiness
Come After Having
Tankards of Ale

Multiplying + and – Numbers

This is a multiplication morality tale courtesy of Rod Evans in Every Good Boy Deserves Fudge.

a) Positive number x positive number = positive

b) Negative number x negative number = positive

c) Positive number x negative number = negative

d) Negative number x positive number = negative

$$\text{a) } 3 \times 4 = 12 \qquad \text{b) } -3 \times -4 = 12$$
$$\text{c) } 3 \times -4 = -12 \qquad \text{d) } -3 \times 4 = -12$$

a) If a good thing happens to a good person, that's good.
b) If a bad thing happens to a bad person, that's good.
c) If a good thing happens to a bad person, that's bad.
d) If a bad thing happens to a good person, that's bad.

Also:
  Minus times minus is plus
  The reason for this we need not discuss.

  Even times even is even
  Odd times even is even
  But odd times odd
  Is always odd.

Order of mathematical calculation

PEMDAS
Please Excuse My Dear Aunt Sally

Parentheses, Exponents, Multiplication, Division, Addition, Subtraction

Calculate things in Parentheses first, then Square Roots and Powers etc (Exponents), then Multiply and Divide, and lastly Add or Subtract.

Eg: $3 \times (5 + 4)^2$
$5 + 4 = 9$, squared $= 81 \times 3 = 243$

BODMAS

Brackets, Orders, Division, Multiplication, Addition, Subtraction.
(Orders means exponents, and multiplication and division are interchangeable).

In the U.S. brackets are parentheses, so the mnemonic is PODMAS

And in Canada, they call brackets brackets, and exponents exponents, so the mnemonic is BEDMAS.

Billions and trillions

This is not a mnemonic, but knowing these big numbers could be mighty useful one day. It's hard to believe, but until around 35 years ago, Britain and the US had differing definitions of what constituted a billion and a trillion. Historically, such numbers were not often encountered outside the world of mathematics and science.

A million seemed to be OK, six noughts, but that's where the agreement ended. Rather worryingly for the international banking system, the US billion was a thousand million (nine noughts) while in Britain billion had meant a million million (12 noughts). Keep up at the back.

It is a testimony to something that the system carried on working despite a discrepancy of a factor of 1,000.

The change in the British definition of a billion came in the Budget statement in 1975 by Chancellor of the Exchequer Denis Healey, who announced that the Treasury would from then on adopt the American version.

The same change affected trillion. The U.S. trillion was a million million, whereas the British version was a million million million. This has now been standardised and a trillion is a million million (12 noughts).
To recap

one million is 6 noughts	1,000,000
one billion is 9 noughts,	1,000 million
one trillion is 12 noughts,	1,000,000 million

The Fibonacci Sequence

The Fibonacci Numbers Sequence works like this:

1+2=3
  2+3=5
    3+5=8   8 + 13 = 21
      5+8=13   13 + 21 = 34
                    21 + 34 = 55
                      34 + 55 = 89

This is a progression in which each term is the sum of the two preceding numbers. Add the last two numbers together to get the next.

1,1, 2, 3, 5, 8, 13, 21, 34, 55, 89, 144, 233, 377, 610, 987, 1,597, 2,584, 4,181, 6,765, 10,946, 17,711, and so on.

Signor Fibonacci, properly Leonardo da Pisa, was born in 1175 to a merchant who later became a customs officer. He travelled widely, and published Liber Abaci (Book of Calculation) in 1202. It was one of the most influential books ever published in mathematics.

It introduced the Latin-speaking world to the Arabic-Hindu numerals 1, 2, 3, 4, 5, 6, 7, 8, 9, plus zero (the Venetian dialect for zefiro, the Latinized word for the Arabic zephirum). Today, he is best known for this simple series of numbers – the Fibonacci Sequence named in his honour.

The ratio of each pair of Fibonacci numbers 5/3; 8/5; 13/8; 21/13 etc approaches a constant – 1.6180339887 and is called the Golden Ratio and Golden Number, known simply as phi - Φ - with numerous applications in nature and science.

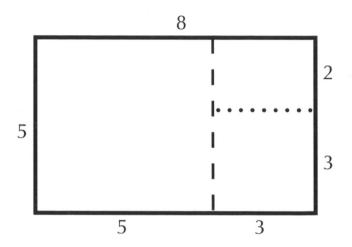

The Golden Ratio describes a rectangle where the longer side is Φ times (1.618) longer than the shorter side.

If the rectangle is 8cm long and 5cm on the shorter side, it would form an approximation of the Golden Rectangle. It can be divided into a square (of 5cm) and a rectangle of 5cm by 3cm, which is also an approximation of the proportion of the golden ratio.

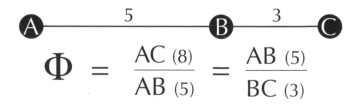

Phi demonstrates some interesting properties:
To square it you just add 1.
$\Phi = 1.618^2 = 2.618$

To get the reciprocal, you just subtract 1.
$1 / \Phi = 0.618$

The Golden Ratio was first described by Euclid around 300BC, although it may have originated in Ancient Egypt. There have been many references to the Ratio through history: the Parthenon was said to have been designed on the principle. Leonardo da Vinci made use of it, as did Le Corbusier. The pattern also occurs in nature.

Flowers follow Fibonacci: buttercups and potatoes have five petals, roses and delphiniums 8, daisies 13 and 21, asters 21 and Michaelmas daisies are said to have 55 or 89 petals. I've never counted them. All are Fibonacci numbers.

The dimensions of the screen of the Mac laptop I am writing this on are almost the same as the Golden Ratio, as are a standard postcard, a standard credit card and a 35mm photographic negative. Also this book laid on its side. And George Clooney's good looks, apparently.

Alan Turing, who is credited with inventing modern computing, studied the patterns of sunflower heads in 1952 seeking to explain Fibonacci phyllotaxis, the name give to links between plant structures and the Fibonacci Sequence. In 2012, an international research project at the Museum of Science and Industry in Manchester based on his research, showed that 82% of sunflower heads analysed had their seeds arranged in a spiral pattern according to the Fibonacci Sequence.

Fibonacci's Rabbits

This was one of the puzzles in Fibonacci's book – a little teaser for schoolchilden 800 years ago. Oh, and it was in Latin.

> How many pairs of rabbits can be produced in one year from a single pair, if each pair produces a new pair every month; each new pair starts reproducing a new pair at the age of one month; and no rabbits die?

Fibonacci assumed that the first pair of rabbits were mature animals and therefore bred in the first month.

1 pair on Jan 1, the pair breeds.

2 pairs at start of Feb:	1 pair breeds
3 pairs at start of March:	2 pairs breed
5 pairs at start of April:	3 pairs breed
8 pairs at start of May:	5 pairs breed
13 pairs at start of June:	8 pairs breed
21 pairs at start of July:	13 pairs breed
34 pairs at start of Aug:	21 pairs breed
55 pairs at start of Sept:	34 pairs breed
89 pairs at start of Oct:	55 pairs breed
144 pairs at start of Nov:	89 pairs breed
233 pairs at start of Dec:	144 pairs breed

meaning that at midnight on December 31 we can expect 377 pairs of rabbits.

The sequence is Fibonacci. At the start of Year 3, we will be on Fibonacci Number 26, which is 121,393. If you grow brassicas and lettuce in your vegetable patch, you will be horrified to learn that at the start of Year 5, we will be on Fibonacci Number 50, which means

$12,586,269,025$ pairs of rabbits.

The Nine Complement

This is a wonderful numbers game, guaranteed to break the ice at parties.

Ask someone for a number between 1 and 999

567

Ask them for another

382

Then repeat the first number

567

and then give your own number. This will be the nine complement of 382 – in this instance 617. Added together the two numbers make 999.

The calculation you are going to do is this:

(567 x 382) = 216,594

plus

(567 x 617) = 349,839

Answer = **566,433**

The quick way goes like this:

567 minus one

566

The nine complement of 566

433

Answer = **566,433**

Go on then, check it out.

And try this one:

(287 x 748) + (287 x 251)

287 minus 1

286

The nine complement of 286

713

Answer = **286,713**

Magic!

The Rule of 72

This is a rough and ready way to estimate how long it takes for an investment to double in value given an average rate of interest. The formula is:

Time = 72/rate of interest

For example, an investment paying 6 per cent per annum would double in 72/6 = 12 years. It's quick and easy and remarkably accurate. When you do the calculation on the proper compound interest formula, the answer comes out as 11 years 327 days.

At a rate of 4 per cent, the time taken for the investment to double would be 72/4 = 18 years. The 72 Rule over-estimates the time needed by 120 days (at least it gives you a nice surprise when it comes) and at 8 per cent (72/8), the estimate of 9 years underestimates the time by three days – remarkably accurate.

Mode and Mean

MOde = MOst common number

MeAN = Average Number

MEDian = Number in middle.

CHAPTER 5

Times Tables

There is no excuse for not trying to learn your tables: they form the basis of arithmetic and, once you have learned them, they will stay with you for the rest of your life, saving you lots of time – and possibly embarrassment – in the process. As Ian Stewart, Emeritus Professor of Mathematics at Warwick University, put it: 'Anyone trying to learn maths will be at a serious disadvantage if, every time 6 x 7 comes up, he or she hasn't a clue what it is. It will be like trying to ride a bike when you can't remember which bits are the pedals.'

But not everybody finds them easy to learn so here are a few tips and devices, from the 2 times table through to the 20 times table. Don't panic: it's not as bad as all that.

It is a fairly comprehensive list. Breaking numbers down makes things a lot easier and it is good to notice and think about some of the patterns that are thrown up. The 18 times table is quite as easy as the 2 times table, as you will discover later.

Two times table

02, 04, 06, 08, 10
12, 14, 16, 18, 20

2   4   6   8 10

Two do we enumerate

Once you can do the ten calculations from 1 x 2 up to 10 x 2, you will in fact know 20 calculations, because all times table answers are mirrored.

Eg: 2 x 3 = 3 x 2   2 x 5 = 5 x 2

          2 x 7 = 7 x 2   2 x 9 = 9 x 2

Three times table

1 x 3	= **3**		**3**	7 x 3	= **21** (2+1)	**3**
2 x 3	= **6**		**6**	8 x 3	= **24**	**6**
3 x 3	= **9**		**9**	9 x 3	= **27**	**9**
4 x 3	= **12**	(1+2)	**3**	10 x 3	= **30**	**3**
5 x 3	= **15**	(1+5)	**6**	11 x 3	= **33**	**6**
6 x 3	= **18**	(1+8)	**9**	12 x 3	= **36** (3+6)	**9**

In the four groups of three numbers 1,2,3; 4,5,6; 7,8,9; 10,11,12; the digit sum of each answer in each group has a pattern of 3,6,9. After 12 x 3, the 3,6,9 pattern continues: just add the products together

Eg:

17 x 3 = 51: 5 + 1 = **6**

1,486 x 3 = 4,458 : 4 + 4 + 5 + 8 = 21: 2 + 1 = **3**

Four times table

If you struggle here, it's probably best to multiply by two, and then again, and add them up. All products will be even numbers.

$1 \times 4 = 2 + 2 = 4$ ($1 \times 2 = 2$, and again $= 4$)

$2 \times 4 = 4 + 4 = 8$ ($2 \times 2 = 4$, and again $= 8$)

$3 \times 4 = 6 + 6 = 12$ ($3 \times 2 = 6$, and again $= 12$)

$4 \times 4 = 8 + 8 = 16$ ($4 \times 2 = 8$, and again $= 16$)

$5 \times 4 = 10 + 10 = 20$ ($5 \times 2 = 10$, and again $= 20$)

Five times table

5, 10, 15, 20, 25, 30, 35, 40, 45, 50

Odd numbers x 5 end in 5

Even numbers x 5 end in 0

Six times table

A similar pattern to the three times table.

1 x 6 = 6	**6**	7 x 6 = 42	**6**
2 x 6 = 12	**3**	8 x 6 = 48	**3***
3 x 6 = 18	**9**	9 x 6 = 54	**9**
4 x 6 = 24	**6**	10 x 6 = 60	**6**
5 x 6 = 30	**3**	11 x 6 = 66	**3**
6 x 6 = 36	**9**	12 x 6 = 72	**9**

*(4+8=12: 1+2=**3**)

In the four groups of three numbers 1,2,3; 4,5,6; 7,8,9; 10,11,12; the sum of each answer in each group has the pattern 6,3,9.

If you multiply any even number by 6, the answer ends in the same even number:

Eg: **2** x 6 = 1**2**   1**6** x 6 = 9**6**

1,46**8** x 6 = 8,80**8**

12,345,67**8** x 6 = 74,074,06**8**

65

6, 7, 8, 9,10 times tables

This is a system that works for the 6, 7, 8, 9 and 10 times tables, but only for the 25 calculations above 6.

ie:

6 x 6 to 6 x 10

7 x 6 to 7 x 10

8 x 6 to 8 x 10

9 x 6 to 9 x 10

10 x 6 to 10 x 10

It's a bit complicated at first and looks it too, but is remarkably easy and extremely interesting once you know how to do it. I am indebted to Dr Margaret Devereux for telling me the system. This is very much a back-up system if you forget your tables, but it throws up some interesting features, not the least being that it introduces the concept of multiplication by 0 and 1. Nonetheless, it should only take a couple of minutes to get the hang of it. Here goes.

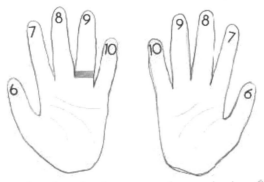

Hold your hands out palms upwards, numbering digits
on the left hand from the thumb 6,7,8,9,10 and digits
on the right hand from the thumb 6,7,8,9,10.

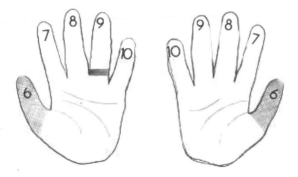

6 x 6

Thumb on left hand, thumb on right hand. At this first
stage of the calculation, these digits count as 10 each,
so count 10 on left and 10 on right = 20. It looks as
if this is not going to work but wait for this: multiply
remaining fingers :

4 on left hand and 4 on right hand   4 x 4 = 16.

    6 x 6 = 20 + 16 = **36**

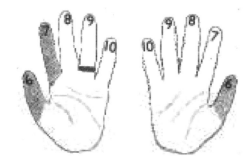

7 x 6

Show thumb (6) and first finger (7) on left hand and thumb (6) on right hand. It's best to pinch multiple digits together – it makes it a bit easier to count them. At this first stage, these digits each count as 10 – therefore 20 on left hand and 10 on the right, making 30. Multiply the three remaining fingers of the left hand with the four remaining fingers of the right hand 3 x 4 = 12

7 x 6 = 30 + 12 = **42**

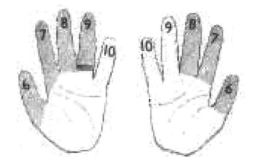

9 x 8

Touch together digits 6,7,8,9, on left hand (40) and digits 6,7,8, on right hand (30), making 70. One finger on left hand multiplied by two fingers on right hand makes 2.

9 x 8 = 70 + 2 = **72**

9 x 9

Digits 6, 7, 8, 9 touching on both hands, each digit counts 10 = 80. Then it gets interesting. Multiply remaining fingers of each hand: 1 x 1 = 1.

$$9 \times 9 = 80 + 1 = \textbf{81}$$

7 x 10

OK, forget the fact that you know the answer – this is to demonstrate the workings of the system and also to introduce the 0 times table.

Digits 6, 7 on left hand and the full five digits on the right hand – each digit counts 10 = 70. This now gets interesting.

Multiply together remaining fingers; 3 on left, 0 on right 3 x 0 = 0.

$$7 \times 10 = 70 + 0 = \textbf{70}$$

This is a very useful system because most people can do the 2x, 3x, 4x, 5x and 10x tables; the only ones they really have trouble with are the 6x, 7x, 8x and 9x tables.

Eight times table

If this causes trouble

Double, double, double

Eg 3 x 8 = **24**

   double 3 = 6

   double 6 =12

   double 12 = **24**

Eg 12 x 8 = **96**

   double 12 = 24

   double 24 = 48

   double 48 = **96**

1 x 8	**8**	**8**
2 x 8	**16**	**7**
3 x 8	24	**6**
4 x 8	**32**	**5**
5 x 8	**40**	**4**
6 x 8	**48**	**3**
7 x 8	56	**2**
8 x 8	64	**1**
9 x 8	72	**9**
10 x 8	80	**8**

Last digits of the products go

8, 6, 4, 2, 0, 8, 6, 4, 2, 0

And the digit sums of the product together give a sequence of:

8, 7, 6, 5, 4, 3, 2, 1, 9, 8

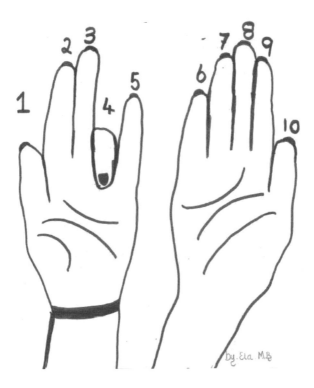

Nine times table

Open hands out palms up.

Number left hand digits from thumb 1,2,3,4,5

and right hand digits from little finger 6,7,8,9,10.

Eg: 4 x 9

Bend down digit 4 . To the left of it are 3 digits, to the right 6 digits.

Answer = **36**

Eg: 7 x 9

Bend digit 7 down. To the left are 6 digits, to the right 3 digits.

Answer = **63**

My daughter loved this – she thought it was the best present we gave her last Christmas. It always works, and only needs the ability to count from one to ten.

It still works at bigger numbers

Eg:14 x 9

10 x 9 (right thumb down, **9** to the left, **0** to the right) = **90**

4 x 9 (fourth finger left hand down, **3** to the left, **6** to the right) = **36**

90 + 36 = **126**

Eg: 452 x 9

Split the calculation up.

400 x 9 = **3,600**   4 x 9 = 36 x 100 = **3,600**

50 x 9 = **450**   5 x 9 = 45 x 10 = **450**

2 x 9 = **18**   2 x 9 = **18**

3,600 + 450 + 18 = **4,068**

The nine times table throws up a number of interesting patterns.

1 x 9 = 9	5 x 9 = 45	9 x 9 = 81
2 x 9 = 18	6 x 9 = 54	10 x 9 = 90
3 x 9 = 27	7 x 9 = 63	11 x 9 = 99
4 x 9 = 36	8 x 9 = 72	12 x 9 = 108

The first five answers are mirrored by the next five

09 18 27 36 45

90 81 72 63 54

And all the products add up to 9. This goes for any number.

Eg: 3 x 9

Answer **27** (2 + 7 = 9)

Eg: 7 x 9

Answer **63** (6 + 3 = 9)

Eg: 28 x 9

Answer **252** (2+5+2 = 9)

Eg: 67,452 x 9

Answer **607,068** (6+7+6+8 = 27: 2+7 = 9)

Eg: 7,683,451 x 9

Answer **69,151,059**

(6 + 9 + 1 + 5 + 1 + 5 + 9 = 36:   3 + 6 = 9)

It really does work:

Eg: 8,356,241,890 x 9: That's more than 8 billion!

Answer **75,206,177,010**

(7+5+2+6+1+7+7+1 = 36: 3+6 = 9)

And how's this for a pretty pattern?

$$1 \times 9 + 9 = 18$$
$$12 \times 9 + 9 = 117$$
$$123 \times 9 + 9 = 1116$$
$$1234 \times 9 + 9 = 11115$$
$$12345 \times 9 + 9 = 111114$$
$$123456 \times 9 + 9 = 1111113$$
$$1234567 \times 9 + 9 = 11111112$$
$$12345678 \times 9 + 9 = 111111111$$

Ten times table

If you can't do the 10 times table, you are probably not going to have understood any of the foregoing, never mind the 11 and 12 times tables still to come. But keep going.

Eleven times table

The only things that I can think of that are counted out in 11s are the number of players in football, cricket and hockey teams and the number of players on the field at any one time for each team in American Football.

An Elfmeter is not something you have to keep feeding with euros to keep the little people heating your house. Elf is the German word for 11 and meter is a meter. It's the German word for penalty kick in football – 10.9728m from the goal. I'm sorry, but 12 yards sounds much sweeter.

The 11 times table is a very interesting one. It's pretty straightforward up to 9.

1 x 11 = 11	6 x 11 = 66
2 x 11 = 22	7 x 11 = 77
3 x 11 = 33	8 x 11 = 88
4 x 11 = 44	9 x 11 = 99
5 x 11 = 55	10 x 11 = 110

It gets more interesting – but just as easy – after that:

Eg: 12 x 11

Take the first number

1   then add the first two numbers $(1 + 2)$

3   then the second number

2

Answer = **132**

Eg: 18 x 11

The first number

   1 then add the first two numbers 1+ 8

   9 then the second number

   8

Answer **198**

Eg: 153 x 11

The first number

   1 Add the first two numbers (1 and 5)

   6 Add the next two numbers (5 and 3)

   8 Then the last number

   3

Answer **1,683**

Eg: 1345 x 11

(1, 1+3, 3+4, 4+5, 5)

Answer = **14,795**

When two numbers added together make 10 or more, just carry it over as in any addition.

Eg: 13,562 x11

1

1+3 = **4**

3+5 = 8 (+1) = **9**

5+6 =11 (this turns the 8 above into 9) remainder **1**

6+2 = **8**

2

Answer **149,182**

This a strange thing I found on the internet. Take any number – write it forwards and then backwards:

456 654

This will be a multiple of 11.

41,514 x 11

(using the method we have just learned).

456,654

Twelve times table

Both the 11 times and 12 times tables have lost some of their relevance in these decimal days. There are no longer 12 pennies in a shilling, but there are 12 inches in a foot, eggs are still sold in dozens and half-dozens, there are 12 hours on a clock face, 12 months in a year, 12 Apostles, 12 people on a jury and we still celebrate the Twelve Days of Christmas.

This is still an important table and is another one that is best learned by heart.

A simple way to get there if you don't know the table is:

Multiply by 2, then by 10, and then add up them up.

Eg: 4 x 12
     4 x 2 = 8
     4 x 10 = 40
     40 + 8 = **48**

Eg: 8 x 12
     8 x 2 = 16
     8 x 10 = 80
     80+16 = **96**

But there is a pattern to the 12 times table. The last digits of the products go 2, 4, 6, 8, 0, 2, 4

1 x 12 = 12	**2**
2 x 12 = 24	**4**
3 x 12 = 36	**6**
4 x 12 = 48	**8**
5 x 12 = 60	**0**
6 x 12 = 72	**2**
7 x 12 = 84	**4**
8 x 12 = 96	**6**
9 x 12 = 108	**8**
10 x 12 = 120	**0**
11 x 12 = 132	**2**
12 x 12 = 144	**4**

Thirteen times table

This may look horrendous, but it isn't. Just break the numbers down.

Times 3, then times 10, then add together.

Eg: 6 x 13   Eg: 23 x 13

    6 x 3 = 18   23 x 3 = 69

    6 x 10 = 60   23 x 10 = 230

   60 + 18 = **78**   230 + 69 = **299**

Fourteen times table

Times 7, then double (or use the 7x table fingers system)

Eg: 8 x 14

    8 x 7 = 56 x 2 = **112**

Or times 4, then times 10, then add them up.

Eg: 8 x 14

    8 x 4 = 32
    8 x 10 = 80
  80 + 32 = **112**

Fifteen times table

Multiply number by 10. Then multiply number by 5

(Or halve the first number)

Then add them together

Eg: 17 x 15

    (17 x 10) = 170

    (17 x 5) = 85

    170 + 85 = **255**

Eg: 17 x 15

    (17 x 10) = 170

    (170 ÷ 2) = 85

    170 + 85 = **255**

Eg: 2,840 x 15

    (2,840 x 10) = 28,400

    + (28,400 ÷ 2) = 14,200

    28,400 + 14,200 = **42,600**

In the second part of the calculation, it will be easier to multiply by 5 in some instances, and to halve the first number in others, especially when the numbers are large. It amounts to the same thing – just choose whichever is easier.

Sixteen times table

Times 8, then double

or better still, use the alternative method:

Times 10, halve it, add together, then add number you started with (the multiplicand).

(I know we are trying to find neat and easy ways of doing arithmetic, but this second method, with practice, will be a lot easier for most people).

Eg: 43 x 16

Eg: 28 x 16

    43 x 8 – 344

    28 x 8 = 224

    344 x 2 = **688**

    224 x 2 = **448**

Eg 43 x 16

Eg 28 x 16

    43 x 10 = 430

    28 x 10 = 280

    halve it = 215

    halve it = 140

    add 43 =   43

    add 28 =   28

    Total = **688**

    Total = **448**

Seventeen times table

Times 7, then times 10, then add them up

Eg: 15 x 17

$15 \times 7 = 105$
$15 \times 10 = 150$
$105 + 150 = \textbf{255}$

Or

Times 2, times 10, halve last number and add them all up

Eg: 15 x 17

$15 \times 2 = 30$
$15 \times 10 = 150$
$150 \div 2 = 75$

$30 + 150 + 75 = \textbf{255}$

Eighteen times table

There are a number of ways of doing this without reaching for your calculator. The first example just needs knowledge of the two times table, the ten times table and the ability to do one simple subtraction. Most people can do that. The example here of 45 x 18 is not a simple calculation at first sight.

Eg: 45 x 18

Times 2, times 10, subtract first number in answer.

$$45 \times 2 = 90$$

$$90 \times 10 = 900$$

subtract 90

$$900 - 90 = \textbf{810}$$

The first part of the answer is the same amount that is subtracted at the end of the calculation.

Another method is Times 10, then times 8 (or times 4 doubled).

Eg: 45 x 18

$$450 + 360 = \textbf{810}$$

$$450 + (180 + 180) = \textbf{810}$$

Another way is to use the nine times table and double it.

Eg: 45 x 18 (using the hand method)

   40 x 9 = 360

    5 x 9 = 45

   Total = 405

   Double it

  405 x 2 = **810**

Also times 10, minus multiplicand, then double

Eg: 45 x 18

   45 x 10 = 450

 Minus 45 = 405

   Double it

  405 x 2 = **810**

The product of a number multiplied by 18 will add up to 9, just as with the 9 times table.

Nineteen times table

I know this looks horrendous but it isn't – it really is easy. Even easier than the 18 times table. Trust me.

Times 2, times 10, then subtract the multiplicand.

Eg: 12 x 19

12 x 2 = 24

24 x 10 = 240

240 – 12 = **228**

There are other ways of calculating this, but none as easy as this. Basically all it needs is the knowledge of the 2x and 10x tables.

Also

Times 10 plus times 9

Eg: 12 x 19

12 x 10 = 120

12 x 9 = 108

120 +108 = **228**

Twenty times table

Easy peasy: times 2 and then times 10

Eg: 17 x 20

    17 x 2 = 34

    34 x 10 = **340**

Eg: 1,415 x 20

    1,415 x 2 = 2,830

    2,830 x 10 = **28,300**

That's enough times tables – I won't extend the agony Suffice to say that the strategies we have used in the preceding tables can still be used for unwieldy and unlikely numbers.

21 times table

Times 2, times10, add multiplicand

22 times table

Times 11, then double

25 times table

Times 5 plus times 10 twice

27 times table

Easy again, multiply by 9 and then by 3

(You can use 9x fingers system).

CHAPTER 6

Measurements

The world's most widely used system of measurements is the SI (Système International d'Unités), from the French, who adopted the metric system back in 1799. There are seven units in the system, and the three basic and most useful are

> Mass: Kilogram
> Length: Metre
> Time: Second

This section will be interesting and useful for readers young and old.

Older people will be totally at home with the old Imperial system and may struggle on the metric system. Younger readers, however, will be at ease with the metric system, having used it for years at school and may struggle on what is now the old-fashioned Imperial system.

We are still hanging on to some of the Imperial units, like measuring distances in yards and miles as they do in America. It seems strange to say 800 metres instead of half a mile. I live 250 miles from London – I would never think of saying 400 kilometres.

It will be interesting to see how many of the Imperial measures survive, but some will. Pints of beer are still alive and well, although gallons long ago lost the forecourt war to litres.

But a 45.44 litre hat doesn't have the same ring as a 10-gallon hat, and 'Beckham looks dangerous on the edge of the 16.4592 metre box' (instead of the 18-yard box) just sounds daft.

Please note:
All the calculations that follow are both quick and approximate.

Kilograms, pounds
Grams, ounces

1,000 grams = 1 kilogram
1 kilogram = 2.2 lbs
1,000 kilograms = 1 tonne

1 ounce (oz) = 28 grams
8 oz = half a pound = 227 grams
1lb = 454 grams

So what weighs one gram? One book I referred to stated quite categorically that a grain of rice weighed one gram. Sorry, but I didn't believe that, and a thorough five-minute empirical investigation (of the basmati rice in the kitchen cupboard) concluded that it needed 40 grains to make up one gram – meaning that our grains of rice weighed in at 25 milligrams each.

On the very day that I made this great discovery, I found out that the mass of the earth – its weight to non-scientists – is 5.97g x 10^{27}. That's 25 noughts after 597: in kilograms, it is 5.97 x 10^{24} (22 noughts after 597). That's a lot of grains of rice.

More comparisons:

A 10mm slice of butter from a normal packet weighs 25g. A packet of butter that we used to call half a pound weighs 250g, which is around 10% more than half a pound.

 A tin of baked beans weighs 415g.

1 kilogram = 1 bag of sugar.

1 tonne = 1 cubic metre of sand from the builders' merchants.
Or a small car like a Fiat Cinquecento or Ford Ka.
And a 15 inch cube of gold.

Ounces to grams

3 and 10

Multiply number of ounces by 3, then by 10

Eg: 8oz x 3 = 24 x 10 = 240g
Exact weight   227g

Grams to ounces

Divide by 3, then divide by 10

Eg: 120g ÷ 3 = 40 ÷ 10 = 4oz
Exact weight   4.233oz

Kilograms to pounds

Times 2 + 10%

Multiply number of kg by 2, then add 10%

Eg: 2.5kg
2.5 x 2 = 5. Add 10% of 5lb = 0.50 = 5.5lb.
Exact weight   5.512lb

This is a useful conversion when you are roasting
a good-sized chicken and need to cook it for 20
minutes a pound.

100 kg = 200 + 20 = 220lb (15 and a half stone – a
good-sized man).

Pounds to kilograms

2lb of apples = 0.9kg
Exact weight   0.908kg
5lb of potatoes = 2.3kg
Exact weight   2.27kg

British coins

In current British coinage, the smaller coins are in ratio both to their value and their weight.

1 x 1p weighs 3.56g
1 x 2p weighs 7.12g
meaning that 2 x 1p weigh the same as 1 x 2p,
as well as being worth the same.

This is very useful and time-saving for bank tellers. It means that a £1 bag of mixed bronze coins (1p and 2p) will weigh 356g irrespective of how many 1p and 2p coins are in the bag. The teller has merely to weigh it rather than count its contents. If the bag weighs 356g, it will contain a total of £1. If it weighs 352.44g, you will be 1p short.

Similarly with 5p and 10p:

1 x 5p weighs 3.25g
1 x 10p weighs 6.50g
meaning again that 2 x 5p weigh the same as 1 x 10p,
as well as being worth the same.

Whatever the make-up of a £5 bag of mixed silver coins (5p and 10p), if the bag weighs 325g, it will contain a total of £5. If it weighs 318.5g, you are either two 5ps or one 10p short.
The sequence stops there.
1 x 20p weighs 5g
1 x 50p weighs 8g
1 x £1 coin weighs 9.50g

Kilometres, miles
Metres, yards
Centimetres, inches

10 millimetres = 1 centimetre
100 centimetres = 1 metre
1,000 metres = 1 kilometre
1 kilometre = 0.6214 miles

1 inch = 2.54cm
1 metre = 39.37in

1 yard = 36 inches = 91.44cm
1 mile = 1.609km

1 cm = average length of a little finger finger-nail.
2 cm = diameter of a 5p piece.
1 metre = height of hip-bone from floor for average sized man. Also the average height of door handles.
Kitchen units have a standard height of 900mm, which is just under 3ft.
400m = one lap of an athletics track.
1 kilometre = a five furlong horse race almost exactly – one kilometre is just seven yards shorter than five furlongs.

The length of the Epsom Derby (one mile and four furlongs) is 2.414km.
1 kilometre = one 15-minute walk.

Inches to centimetres

5 and 2

Multiply number of inches by 5 and divide by 2:

Eg: 6 inches:
    6 x 5 = 30 ÷ 2 = 15cm
    Exact measurement   15.24cm

    12 inches = 1 foot = 30.5cm
    Exact measurement   30.48cm

Feet to metres

Divide by 3, and then subtract 10%

Eg: 6ft:

    6 ÷ 3 = 2 metres

    2 metres minus 10% (0.2 metres) = 1.8 metres.

    Exact measurement   1.8288 metres.

A metre measures three foot three.
It's longer than a yard, you see.

Metres and yards

One area which has gone totally metric worldwide is athletics, where metres and kilometres have totally taken over from yards and miles. Usain Bolt runs the 100 and 200 metres, not the 100 or 220 yards.

There is not much difference between the 400m and the 440 yards as it used to be – it's three yards shorter, but there are differences in the distance events: the 1,500m, which has usurped the One Mile race, is 120 yards shorter – the whole of the finishing straight and a bit. On the other hand, the 10,000m is some 350 yards longer than the Imperial race, the Six Miles, that it replaced.

The marathon is still hanging on at 26 miles 385 yards (or in the metric system 42.195km). The length of the marathon was fixed at the 1908 London Olympics. The race started at Windsor Castle and finished in the White City Stadium, now the site of BBC White City at Shepherd's Bush. To enable Queen Alexandra to get the best view of the end of the race, it was decided that the marathon would finish in front of the Royal Box, which meant that the race was exactly 26 miles and 385 yards long. In 1924 that became the official distance and has remained so since.

Miles to kilometres

5 and 8

Divide by 5 and multiply by 8

Eg: 10 miles is 16 km

Exact distance...16.9034km

One kilometre is 0.6214 of a mile.

Kilometres to miles

8 and 5

Divide by 8 and multiply by 5.

Eg: 24 km is 15 miles.

24÷8 = 3 x 5 = 15 miles

Exact distance   14.9136 miles

This is a simple conversion and appears to be reasonably accurate.

The number of kilometres is always more than miles because kilometres are shorter than miles.

For converting Miles and Kilometres, look back at the section on the Fibonacci Numbers on Page 53. Basically you only have to remember two numbers – 2 and 3. Added together, this gives the next number in the sequence: 5.

5km is 3 miles   *(Exact 3.107 miles)*
 Add 5 and 3 = 8
8km is 5 miles   *(Exact 4.97 miles)*
 Add 5 and 8 = 13
13km is 8 miles   *(Exact 8.078 miles)*
 Add 8 and 13 = 21
21km is 13 miles   *(Exact 13.01 miles)*
And so on.
 Add 13 and 21 = 34
34km is 21 miles   *(Exact 21.126 miles)*
 Add 21 + 34 = 55
55km is 34 miles   *(Exact 34.175 miles)*
A continental speed limit
 of 55kph equates to 34mph).
 Add 34 + 55 = 89 .
89km is 55 miles   *(Exact 55.3 miles)*

(A speed limit of 80kph equates to 50mph).

Volume

Volume describes how much space a three-dimensional object takes up.

1,000 millilitres = 100 centilitres = 1 litre
Think of one litre of milk.

1 pint = 568 millilitres

1 litre = 1.7597 pints

A litre of water's
A pint and three quarters

1 cubic cm of water = 1 gram
1 litre of water = 1kg
1 cubic metre of water = 1 tonne

Two litres is a large Coke or Pepsi bottle. Also the volume of the combustion chambers of a 2,000cc (cubic centimetres) car engine.

A bottle of wine = 75cl (three-quarters of a litre)

An average can of Coke = 330ml (one-third of a litre)

Pints and Litres

4 and 7

Pints to litres

Multiply by 4, divide by 7
1 pint = 568 ml   (0.568 of a litre)
Eg: 5 pints
    5 x 4 = 20 ÷ 7 = 2.86 litres
        Exact volume 2.84 litres

Litres to pints

Multiply by 7 and divide by 4
1 litre = 1.7597 pints
Eg: 10 litres
    10 x 7 = 70 ÷ 4 = 17.5 pints
        Exact volume 17.597 pints
The number of pints is always more than the number
of litres because a pint is smaller than a litre.

Gallons to litres

9 and 2
Multiply by 9, divide by 2

Eg: 5 gallons x 9 = 45 ÷ 2 = 22.5 litres
            Exact volume 22.73 litres

1 gallon = 8 pints
Weighs 10lb.

Litres to gallons

Multiply by 2, divide by 9

Eg: 50 litres x 2 = 100 ÷ 9 = 11.1gallons.

The exact answer is along the lines of:
11.111111111111111111111111111111111111111111111
111111111111111111111111111111111111111111111111
111111111111111111111111111111111111111111111111
recurring

1 gallon = 4.546 litres.

5 litres is 1.111 gallons recurring.

A pint's a pound in America all round,

But a pound and a quarter of British water.

An Imperial liquid pint is 20 fluid ounces, an American pint 16 fl oz.

1 fl oz = 29.5ml

Spoons

One big T equals teaspoons three

One tablespoon (15ml) = three teaspoons (5ml).

In the US, the volume of a teaspoon is 4.9289ml.

Depth of a fathom

Six letters,

Six feet.

Mark Twain took his pen name from the word for two fathoms (twain), the minimum navigable depth of the Mississippi, where he worked at one time piloting riverboats.

Area

I have been surprised while working on this book by the number of people, intelligent, educated, who have happily told me they have no idea what constitutes an acre, even though they may remember that it is 4,840 square yards. I am not surprised, however, about most people's ignorance about its metric relation, the hectare.

It is worth getting clear first how area is measured:

Nine square yards is an area bounded by sides 3 yards long (or the equivalent – say 4 yd x 2.25 yd or 9 yd x 1 yd).
Nine square yards is not an area bounded by sides 9 yards long – that would be an area of 81 square yards.
This makes a big difference if you are buying carpet and could save you a lot of money.

9 sq yd = 9 sq yd

9 yd sq = 81 sq yd

10 sq m = 10 sq m

10 m sq = 100 sq m

An acre is 4,840 square yards, and was first limited by statute as long ago as 1277 by Edward I, and then later by Edward III in 1358 and Henry VIII in 1533.

It was based on the average amount of land that could be ploughed in a single day with oxen and was calculated to be a furlong (furrow long) in distance (220 yards) and one chain (22 yards) wide.
220 yd x 22 yd = 4,840 sq yd.

A hectare is a much more clinical area: 100m square.

1 acre = 4,840 sq yds = 0.4046 hectares.

1 hectare = 10,000 sq m = 2.47 acres.

1 sq mile = 640 acres = 259 hectares.

Acres to hectares

Multiply by 0.4

Hectares to acres

Multiply by 2.5

The easiest way to visualise an acre is to think of a Premiership football pitch, the average length being 110 yards and the average width 75 yards. So if you are standing behind the goals at one end, an acre is the half of the pitch up to the halfway line and then into the opponents' half, say 12 – 15 yards, just past the edge of the centre circle.

The biggest pitch in the Premiership – 116 yds x 77 yds – is Manchester City's, followed closely by

Manchester United, which is one yard narrower, and then (when they are in the Premier League) Blackburn Rovers, one yard shorter. The average area is around 1.75 acres. FIFA standardised the dimensions of pitches for internationals in 2007 at 105m x 68m which is just about 115 yds x 74 yds and exactly the dimensions of the pitch at the new Wembley Stadium. The difference between the area of the biggest pitch (Manchester City, 8,932 sq yd), and the smallest West Ham (7,700 sq yd), is 1,200 sq yd, a quarter of an acre.

Richter Scale

The Richter Scale goes from one to ten and measures the magnitude of earthquakes. It is based on a logarithmic scale (base 10), which means that one unit on the scale represents a 10-fold increase in the magnitude of the earthquake. So an earthquake of magnitude 7 is (10^1) ten times bigger than an earthquake of magnitude 6.

The difference in intensity of an earthquake of magnitude 7 and one of magnitude 5 is $(7 - 5 = 2)$ 10^2 = 100.

The earthquake and tsunami in Japan in 2011 registered 8.9, a massive quake. In theory the scale has no upper limit, but in practice, no earthquake has ever measured above magnitude 9.

Shoe sizes

It may be hard to believe, but British shoe sizes today are rooted in a measurement system at least 700 years old. The scheme was formalised towards the end of the reign of Edward II in 1324, and was based on the size of a barleycorn. Three barleycorns placed side by side measured an inch, each barleycorn being one-third of an inch. So shoe sizes increased in increments of one-third of an inch. And they still do.

Today, Size 8 is one-third of an inch bigger than Size 7 and one-third of an inch smaller than Size 9, the average UK men's size. The difference in size between Size 7 and Size 10 is one inch – the whole three barleycorns.

Incidentally, it appears that Edward II had quite big feet himself, which might explain his interest in the subject. He was a Size 12, which in fact is just over a foot. . .

Decibels

Noise is measured in decibels. For each 10 points of the scale, there is a 10-fold increase in sound intensity. On the dB scale the smallest audible sound is 0dB. A sound ten times louder is 10dB. 20dB is a sound (10^2) 100 times louder.

30 dB is $10 \times 10 \times 10$ (10^3) = 1,000 times more powerful than silence.

Normal conversation is around 60db, a hair dryer 90, a lawnmower comes in at 90, a chainsaw 110, a rock concert is 120dB and a jet engine is 130dB at take-off from 200ft.

Maria Sharapova's grunt was measured at 103.2dB at Wimbledon 2011, although her record set in 2009 was 105dB, as loud as a pneumatic drill.

There is an alarm clock on the market that proudly advertises that its ring is 113dB. This is guaranteed to do two things: get you out of bed, and give you permanent hearing damage very quickly.

Paper sizes

Standard paper sizes are used in most countries in the world today. In the ISO 216 paper size system, the aspect-ratio of height-to-width for all sizes is $\sqrt{2}$ to 1. $\sqrt{2} = 1.4142$, so the ratio is 1.4142 : 1.

Start with a sheet of A4. Fold parallel to its shorter side and you will have two sheets of A5 of the same aspect ratio of 1.4142 : 1.

Fold the sheet of A5 parallel to its shorter side again, and you will have two sheets of A6 of the same aspect-ratio but smaller, roughly the size of a postcard.

The series generally starts with paper size A0, which has an area of one square metre, with dimensions of 841mm x 1189mm. Folded in half you get two sheets of 594mm x 841mm. This is size A1. Fold one A1 sheet in half parallel to the shorter side and you get two sheets of A2.

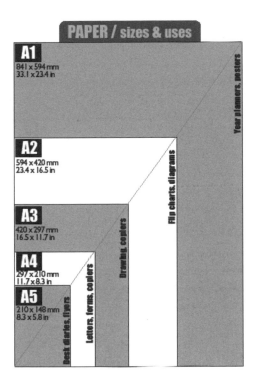

One sheet of A2 folded in half gives a size 297mm x 420mm, which is A3. There will be eight sheets of A3 from the original A0 sheet. Next stop is our beloved A4, which is one sheet of A3 folded in half to make a size of 210mm x 297mm. There will be 16 sheets of A4 from the original A0 sheet.

Moving further down the series, the shorter side of the larger size beomes the longer side of the smaller size.

Eg: Shorter side of A3 (297mm) becomes longer side of A4 (297mm).

It is an extremely effective and efficient system, not least in photocopying. If you put two A4 pages side by side and reduce copying by 71% both pages will fit exactly on one sheet of A4 paper. (71% is half the aspect-ratio of 1.414).

Most countries in the world use the system, except for the US.

How much does a sheet of A4 paper weigh? Well it depends on the quality of the paper, but say it weighs $80g/m^2$, which is the default weight for paper you buy at the supermarket. As we have seen above, you get 16 A4 pages from one A0 sheet (which is 1sq m). Therefore each sheet of A4 paper weighs (80g/16), which is 5 grams. The Royal Mail weight limit for ordinary mail is 100g, so you would easily get a good 10 sheets of paper in your envelope and still be well inside the weight limit.

The ISO formats have many uses apart from office paper. Playing cards are A7, and, should you want to know, the single sheets of many brands of toilet paper in Germany are format A6.

CHAPTER 7

History

This is a long-standing classic rhyme for remembering the Kings and Queens of England, and if you can be bothered to learn it by rote, it will definitely come in useful one day.

Willie, Willie, Harry, Stee,
Harry, Dick, John, Harry Three,
One, Two, Three Neds, Richard Two,
Harry Four, Five, Six. Then who?
Edward Four, Five, Dick the Bad,
Harrys Twain and Ned Six the Lad.
Mary, Bessie, James the Vain,
Charlie, Charlie, James again,
William and Mary, Anna Gloria,
Four Georges, William and Victoria,
Edward Seventh next and then,
George the Fifth in 1910.
Edward the Eighth soon abdicated
So another George was reinstated.
After which, Elizabeth,
That's all folks, until her death.

Lineal descent of the British Royal Family:

This table showing the lineal descent of the sovereigns of Great Britain is from the 1840 edition of Dr WB Richard Gray's A First Book in Chronology. It is a useful and simple visual exposition.

Key

•The sovereigns are printed in capitals; those through whom the succession was conveyed are in italics.

•A vertical line **I** indicates immediate descent. (Thus Richard I was the son of Henry II).

•A horizontal line — indicates that those connected by it were children of the same parent. (Thus Edward VI, Mary and Elizabeth were brothers and sisters, the children of Henry VIII).

•Names connected by a bracket } indicate marriage.

•Names connected by = indicate matrimonial alliances. Thus the entry for Charles I: Charles II, James II and Mary were his children. Mary married William Prince of Orange and they had a son also called William. James II had a daughter Mary, who married William, whose succession as William III was established by his being both nephew and son-in-law of James II.

To bring the chart up to date, Victoria reigned from 1837 to 1901, and was succeeded by her son Edward VII. His son reigned as George V from 1910–36. His son Edward VIII abdicated in 1936 when he insisted on marrying Wallis Simpson, a divorcee. His brother George VI became king in December 1936 – his battle against stammering was later filmed as the Oscar-winning The King's Speech in 2010. George VI's elder daughter became Elizabeth II in 1952.

LINEAL DESCENT OF THE SOVEREIGNS OF ENGLAND,

WILLIAM THE CONQUEROR

Robert—WILLIAM 2nd—HENRY 1st—*Adela*
E. of Blois }

STEPHEN

Matilda
Geoffrey Plantagenet }
Earl of Anjou

HENRY 2nd

RICHARD 1st—JOHN

HENRY 3rd

EDWARD 1st

EDWARD 2nd

EDWARD 3rd

Edward (Black Prince)—*John*—*Edmund*
D. of Lancaster   D. of York
RICHARD 2nd
HENRY 4th   *Richard*
E. of Cambridge
{ *Catherine*=HENRY 5th
{ Owen Tudor
HENRY 6th   *Richard,*
D. of York
Edmund,
E. of Richmond
EDWARD 4th—RICHARD 3rd

HENRY 7th—*Elizabeth*—EDWARD 5th

{ *Margaret*   *Mary,*—HENRY 8th
{ *James 4th*   D. of Suffolk
{ of Scotland   EDWARD 6th—MARY—ELIZABETH
Lady Jane Grey

Mary of Guise

Mary Queen of Scots

JAMES 1st

Elisabeth—— ——CHARLES 1st
Frederick Pr. Palat. of
the Rhine   CHARLES 2nd—JAMES 2nd— { *Mary*
{ W. Prince of Orange
{ *Sophia*
{ Elector of Brunswick   ANNE——*Mary*—WILLIAM 3rd

GEORGE 1st

GEORGE 2nd

Frederick (Prince of Wales)

GEORGE 3rd

GEORGE 4th—WILLIAM 4th—*Edward,*
Duke of Kent

VICTORIA.

C

House of Normandy: William I (The Conqueror) 1066 – 1087; William II 1087 – 1100; Henry I 1100 – 1135; Stephen 1135 – 1154.

House of Plantagenet: Henry II 1154 –1189; Richard I 1189 – 1199; John 1199 – 1216; Henry III 1216 – 1272; Edward I 1272 – 1307; Edward II 1307 – 1327; Edward III 1327 – 1377; Richard II 1377 – 1399.

House of Lancaster: Henry IV (Duke of Lancaster) 1399 – 1413; Henry V 1413 – 1422; Henry VI 1422 – 1461; 1470 – 1471.

House of York: Edward IV, Duke of York, 1461 – 1470; 1471 –1483; Edward V 1483; Richard III 1483 – 1485.

House of Tudor: Henry VII 1485 –1509; Henry VIII 1509 – 1547; Edward VI 1547 – 1553; Mary I 1553 – 1558; Elizabeth I 1558 – 1603.

House of Stuart: James I 1603 – 1625; Charles I 1625 – 1649.
Commonwealth and Protectorate: 1649 – 1660.

House of Stuart: Charles II 1660 – 1685; James II 1685 – 1688.

House of Orange and Stuart: William III 1689 – 1702, (his wife Mary II 1689 – 1695); Anne 1702 – 1714.

House of Hanover: George I 1714 –1727; George II 1727 – 1760; George III 1760 – 1820; George IV 1820 – 1830; William IV 1830 – 1837; Victoria 1837 – 1901.

House of Saxe-Coburg-Gotha, Windsor from 1917: Edward VII 1901 – 1910; George V 1910 – 1936; Edward VIII 1936; George VI 1936 – 1952; Elizabeth II 1952 –

The Royal Houses of England

No Plan Like Yours To
Study History So Wisely

Normandy 1066; Plantagenet 1154; Lancaster 1399;
York 1461; Tudor 1485; Stuart 1603 – 1649, 1660;
Hanover 1714; Saxe-Coburg-Gotha 1901; Windsor
1917 –

Red Rose, White Rose

The White Rose of York and Yorkshire

W is near Y in the alphabet

The Red Rose of Lancaster and Lancashire

This is the other one.

Also Manchester United and Liverpool play in red;

Leeds United play in white.

Henry VIII's wives

Henry VIII had six wives and this famous rhyme describes their respective fates.

Divorced, beheaded, died
Divorced, beheaded, survived

Catherine of Aragon	m 1510
Anne Boleyn	m 1533
Jane Seymour	m 1536
Anne of Cleves	m 1540
Catherine Howard	m 1540
Catherine Parr	m 1543

Kate and Anne and Jane.
And Anne and Kate (again, again)

Aragon, Boleyn, Seymour
Cleves, Howard, Parr

Able Bodied Seaman
Clobbered Hairy Pirate

Cabal

An interesting one this – the mnemonic for Charles II's five chief ministers. I can't think of a situation in which it will come in useful, but you never know.

The Shorter Oxford Dictionary has an entry for Cabal dated 1646: a private intrigue of a sinister character formed by a small body of persons. There is another entry dated 1660: a small body of persons engaged in private machination or intrigue.

So it was that in 1670, 24 years after the word had been noted and recorded, Charles II's ministers, viz

Clifford, Arlington, Buckingham, Ashley Cooper and Lauderdale,

signed the Secret Treaty of Dover with France.

The initials of the five ministers' names make up the word Cabal. Spooky.

Battles:

13B, 14A, 15F:

Bannockburn 1314

Agincourt 1415

Flodden 1513

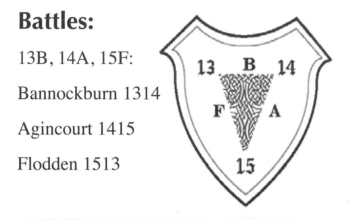

Wars of the Roses

A Boy Now Will Mention All The Hot, Horrid Battles Till Bosworth

St Albans (1455), Blore Heath, Northampton, Wakefield, Mortimer's Cross, Second Battle of St Albans, Towton, Hedgeley Moor, Hexham, Barnet, Tewkesbury, Bosworth (1485).

War of the Spanish Succession

Use the Duke of Marlborough's phone number:

BROM 4689

Blenheim 1704, Ramillies 1706, Oudenarde 1708, Malplaquet 1709.

The Gunpowder Plot

Remember, remember,
The Fifth of November,
Gunpowder, treason and plot.
I see no reason
Why gunpowder treason
Should ever be forgot.

Everybody knows this old rhyme celebrating the foiling of a Catholic plot by Guy Fawkes and others to blow up the Houses of Parliament on November 5, 1605.

King James I ordered that the event should be commemorated and celebrated every year, and commissioned an annual Gunpowder Plot sermon by a leading churchman. It is quite probable that the mnemonic dates from around that time.

Bonfire Day became a legal holiday, celebrated with fireworks and the burning of effigies of Guy Fawkes and, often, the Pope. The holiday lasted for 250 years before being repealed in 1859.

The Great Fire of London

London blazed like kindling sticks
In 1600 and 66.

The Hundred Years' War

So how long did it last? Correct:116 years. The mnemonic for this is: add up the number of letters and spaces (ignore punctuation) in Hundred Years' War (16) and add it to the first word you started with, 100. Alternatively, just remember 116. The war between England and France started in 1337 and was deemed to have ended in 1453. The 1,000-year Byzantine Empire ended in the same year.

The Spanish Armada

The Spanish Armada met its fate
In 1500 and 88

Here's an interesting one – probably the first BOGOF mnemonic: Buy One, Get One Free.

George III said with a smile,
1760 yards in a mile.

George III acceded to the throne in 1760, and there are 1760 yards in a mile. In today's metric world, there may be more schoolchildren who know that George III became king in 1760 than there are who know how many yards are in a mile.

Oh, and the number of feet in a mile:

Five tomatoes: 5 2 8 0

This is an American mnemonic, and so you have to say to-mayt-oes.

The British Monarchy: Order of Succession

Charlie Windsor Had A Ball

1 Charles

2 William

3 Harry

4 Andrew

5 Beatrice

Eager Eddie Just Lost All

6 Eugenie

7 Edward

8 James, Viscount Severn (b 2007)

9 Louise (Lady Louise Windsor, b 2003)

10 Anne

This was the order of the Royal Succession for the British Monarchy in the early part of 2013. But this was to change with the news that Prince William and Catherine, the Duke and Duchess of Cambridge, were expecting a baby. This baby prince or princess will be

Peter's Sis Is Zara's Link

11 Peter Phillips

12 Savannah Phillips (b 2010)

13 Isla Elizabeth Phillips (b 2012)

14 Zara Phillips

15 Viscount Linley

third in line, being the eldest child of Prince William, who is the eldest child of Prince Charles, who himself was the eldest child of the Queen. Everybody else will have to move down a place.

At present, the crown normally passes from the monarch to the eldest son. If the monarch has no son, the crown passes to the eldest daughter. Under male primogeniture, if the monarch has a number of sons, they all take precedence over any daughters, irrespective of age. And the sons' children take precedence too.

But the law is to change after an announcement in October 2011 at the Commonwealth Heads of Government meeting in Australia that gender had become irrelevant. Prime Minister David Cameron said: 'Attitudes have changed fundamentally over the centuries and some of the outdated rules just don't make any sense any more'.

At the end of 2012, the Cabinet Office was awaiting formal consent from 15 Commonwealth realms, but a spokesman said that change in the law would be backdated to the agreement in principle in Perth. In the House of Commons, the British Government prepared a Succession of the Crown Bill.

In the order of succession at the start of 2013, Princess Beatrice is fifth in line because she is the elder daughter of Prince Andrew, the Queen's younger son. The children of the Queen's youngest son, Prince Edward, James and Louise, are eight and ninth.

Princesses Beatrice and Eugenie don't have any male siblings; Lord Severn takes precedence over his elder sister Louise because he is male. Similarly with Peter Phillips and his sister Zara. Princess Anne's son Peter is 11th in line, and Savannah and Isla, his daughters, are 12th and 13th. Princess Anne's daughter Zara comes 14th.

There have been moves afoot to reform the order of succession for many years. Opponents of the principle of male primogeniture had been pressing for equal rights for women to succeed to the throne, superseding the Act of Settlement 1701. When the law is changed, it will almost certainly mean the repeal of laws excluding Catholics, or those who marry them, from the line of succession.

Geoffrey Robertson, QC, was quoted: 'In order to hold the office of head of state you must be a white Anglo-

German Protestant – a descendant of Princess Sophia of Hanover – down the male line on the feudal principle of primogeniture. This is in blatant contravention of the Sex Discrimination Act and the Human Rights Act.' Quite.

Some years ago Lord Archer, the novelist, unsuccessfully proposed a Bill in the House of Lords abolishing the right of males to take precedence over females in the Royal Succession. Comedian Bob Monkhouse said it was a shame: 'It is the only thing that Jeffrey Archer ever wrote that deserved a second reading.'

In the present Line of Succession, the King of Sweden is 201st in line, and, strangely, the Queen's husband, Prince Philip, is 503rd. A namesake of mine, Robin Bryan (who he?), is 520th in line. He must be from the other side of the family – in fact his father was American and his mother was Lady Iris Mountbatten. There is an intriguing-looking character at 1,264 in the list – Prince Boris of Bulgaria. The British throne is not going to disappear for lack of qualified candidates for the job.

The course of history could have been different if the eldest daughter had been able to become Queen. Queen Victoria's eldest child was a girl, Victoria, who went on to marry Frederick III, Emperor of Germany and King of Prussia. Their eldest son became Kaiser Wilhelm II. Had the young Victoria succeeded her mother, it is possible that Kaiser Wilhelm, the German Emperor generally blamed for starting the First World War, could have acceded to the British throne.

A Cat Eats My Hat.

Which Hat, What Cat?

That's My Burmese Blue Cat!

Attlee, Clement	1945 – 1951
Churchill, Winston	1951 – 1955
Eden, Anthony	1955 – 1957
Macmillan, Harold	1957 – 1963
Home, Alec Douglas	1963 – 1964
Wilson, Harold	1964 – 1970
Heath, Edward	1970 – 1974
Wilson, Harold	1974 – 1976
Callaghan, James	1976 – 1979
Thatcher, Margaret	1979 – 1990
Major, John	1990 – 1997
Blair, Tony	1997 – 2007
Brown, Gordon	2007 – 2010
Cameron, David	2010 –

Roman Emperoz

At The Canine Club, Never Give Out Vile Vegetables To Dalmatians

Augustus	27BC	– 14AD
Tiberius	14AD	– 37AD
Caligula	37AD	– 41AD
Claudius	41AD	– 54AD
Nero	54AD	– 68AD
Galba	68AD	– 69AD
Otho	69AD	
Vitellius	69AD	
Vespasian	69AD	– 79AD
Titus	79AD	– 81AD
Domitian	81AD	– 96AD

CHAPTER 8

Geography

North and South

There are two more contenders here for the most simple mnemonic in the book. The first one comes courtesy of Lord Brocket.

The peer was serving five years at Littlehey Prison in Cambridgeshire for attempted fraud. Life inside was tough for a peer of the realm, but in a letter to the novelist Dame Barbara Cartland he said he had been trying to help some of his fellow inmates, a number of whom were illiterate and innumerate. He said he showed a map of Britain to one inmate, who had no idea what it was.

'As for London, he hadn't a clue. North and South, he had no idea. So I told him:

Nut (Head) for **N**orth and **S**hoes for **S**outh

– and he's got it!' Most people won't need a mnemonic for north and south, but full marks to Lord Brocket in coming up with one which was both meaningful and effective in the situation.

Another mnemonic for north and south, east and west is:

Never Eat Shredded Wheat

Don't really mean that Nestlé! Shredded Wheat is good for you – it is made from just one ingredient: 100% Whole Grain Wheat. Nothing more. Nothing extra. That should keep the Nestlé lawyers happy.

Left and Right

Pretty simple stuff I know.

With your left hand face down, move the thumb 90 degrees away from the index finger. You get the shape of a capital L. This is your Left Hand.

The other one is Not Your Left Hand —The Right Hand.

It's basic I know, but apparently more people than you would think have trouble knowing their right from their left.

It also works in French.

Gauche (Left): make a G with your thumb and first finger on your left hand. Droite (Right): make a D with your thumb and first finger on the right hand.

And German: Link (Left) and the other one, Recht (Right). And it completely works in Welsh too: Chwith (Left) and De (Right).

While we're on the basics, how about this for how to lay the table?

Left......Fork (4 letters)

Right....Knife (5 letters)

Port and Starboard

- We left port and went right to starboard.

- There's some more red port left.

- Port is left – both have four letters.

- Port is always passed to the left round the dinner table.

The seven continents

Eat An Aspirin After
A Night-time Snack

Europe, Antarctica, Asia, Africa,

Australia, North America, South America.

(The second letter in the first three entries beginning with A is another clue).

Longitude and Latitude

LONGitude: Think of great LONG circles running north-south meeting at the Poles. All the circles are the same length. LONGitude is the distance ALONG the Equator measured in degrees from Greenwich.

LATitude is the LATeral distance north or south from the Equator measured in degrees. This could be termed lateral thinking, or sideways across thinking. The circles decrease in size as they move away from the Equator towards the Poles.

The Equator is at Latitude 0 degrees, and the Poles at Latitude 90 degrees. Greenwich, the home of The Royal Observatory in South East London, is at 0 degrees Longitude, and 51.5 degrees North Latitude.

The Equator is the fattest line of latitude at 40,075.16 kilometers.

Tropic of Cancer/Capricorn

CaNcer is North

Capricorn is the other one (South)

At noon on June 21, the sun is directly overhead at latitude 23.5 degrees North – the Tropic of Cancer. This marks the start of summer in the northern hemisphere. On December 21 in the southern hemisphere, the sun is directly overhead at midday at latitude 23.5 degrees South – the Tropic of Capricorn.

365

Mount Fujiyama, the highest mountain in Japan is

12,365 feet

12 months in a year, 365 days in a year.

Lake Malawi is 365 miles long and is known as the Calendar Lake.

Knole, the massive Elizabethan ancestral home in Kent of Robert Sackville-West, the 7th Baron Sackville, is known as a Calendar House: it has, it is said, 365 rooms *(days)*, 52 staircases *(weeks)*, 12 entrances *(months)*, seven courtyards *(days in a week)* spread over four acres *(seasons)*, with a 26-acre walled garden *(half a year)*.

The height of St Paul's Cathedral in London is 365 feet, and would be visible if it was relocated anywhere in the Irish Sea.

The Great Lakes

No collection of mnemonics would be complete without a few concerning the Great Lakes of North America – sometimes I think they are there just to bulk out the collection. So, in the interests of comprehensiveness and bulkiness, here they are:

HOMES:

Huron, Ontario, Michigan, Erie, Superior.

West to East:

Susan Mitchell Has Eight Oranges

Superior, Michigan, Huron, Erie, Ontario.

And this, taught at the Convent of Sacred Heart High School in Hammersmith, London, in the 1940s:

Some Monkeys Hate Eating Oranges

East to West:

Only Elephants Have Massive Snouts

Ontario, Erie, Huron, Michigan, Superior.

By area:

Sam's Horse Must Eat Oats

Superior, Huron, Michigan, Erie, Ontario.

Longest rivers

Rivers change their length all the time, and measuring standards change too, so there is no list that is going to be definitive for ever. When I first wrote this list last year, the Ob-Irtysh was the fifth longest but has now been downgraded to seventh, losing more than 100 miles in the process.

By popular agreement, though, the Nile is the longest river in the world at between 4,132 and 4,180 miles. It rises in Burundi, and with its tributaries, flows through nine countries before reaching the Nile delta and the Mediterranean. The Amazon is the largest river in the world measured by the amount of water that flows down it.

Between 2009 and 2011, the Nile seems to have grown by 100 miles and the Amazon shrunk by 100 miles.

NAY.MY.HO

Nile	4,180 miles	6,693km
Amazon	3,976	6,400
Yangste	3,917	6,300
Mississippi	3,902	6,275
Yenisey	3,445	5,539
Huang He	3,398	5,464
Ob-Irtysh	3,364	5,410

No, I'd never heard of the Yenisey or the Ob-Irtysh either. The Huang He is the Yellow River, so-called after the colour of its silt.

The source of the Yenisey is in central Mongolia and flows south to north through Siberia to the Arctic Ocean. The Ob rises in the Altai Mountains and flows through Siberia to the Gulf of Ob. The Irtysh, which originates in China, is its main tributary, and both these rivers are frozen over for half the year.

All these rivers are just about twice as long as the longest river in Europe, the Danube (1,770 miles). The UK's longest river is the Severn at 222 miles (364km), just ahead of the Thames at 215 miles (346km).

Highest mountains

EK too

Everest	8,850m
K2	8,610m
Kangchenjunga	8,586m

The oceans

Perhaps Aunt Ira
should call the AA

Pacific, Atlantic, Indian, Antarctic, Arctic.

Beverly Hills

Readers will have noticed that the definition of a mnemonic in the book has been pretty wide. Well here's another one.

If we say a mnemonic is an aid to memory, then how about this – the threat of the sack?

When I was in a position of some power on a Sunday newspaper, I made a rule that any sub-editor who allowed Beverly Hills to be spelled incorrectly in the newspaper (as Beverley, the spelling of Hills generally not being a problem) would be sacked on the spot.

I don't know why that particular error bugged me so much, but it did. It may have been that there seemed to be a reference to Beverly Hills on every other page (and these days in almost every other story).

But nobody ever did spell it incorrectly, and therefore nobody was ever summarily dismissed. So the threat of the sack proved to be a very effective aid to memory.

In researching this book, I discovered that Beverly Hills, California, was named at the start of the 20th century after the small town of Beverly and its rolling hills in Massachusetts.

And that the settlement of Beverly, Massachusetts, was named in 1668 – yes you've guessed it – after Beverley in east Yorkshire.

So Beverly itself was a spelling mistake all along. I feel a bit better now that nobody was fired.

And while we are in West Los Angeles . . .

Glenn Close:

Two Ns, the same as Bunny Boiler in Fatal Attraction.

The streets of New York

Eastbound streets are even,

Westbound streets are odd.

Obey the traffic signals,

And leave the rest to God.

And the streets of Seattle

The east - west streets at the heart of the central business district share their first letters. From south to north:

Jesus Christ Made Seattle Under Protest

Jefferson	James
Cherry	Columbia
Marion	Madison
Spring	Seneca
University	Union
Pike	Pine

From Bart Benne's excellent book Waspleg.

The Seven Hills of Rome

(Clockwise from the west)

Can Queen Victoria Eat Cold Apple Pie?

Capitoline, Quirinal, Viminal, Esquiline,

Caelian, Aventine, Palatine.

Some local mnemonics:

The Rivers of Yorkshire

Surely Una Never Was A Careful Driver

Swale, Ure, Nidd, Wharfe, Aire, Calder, Don

Stoke-upon-Trent

Two Brown Hats Sell For Less

You're not going to get this one easily. It was taught (among other things I'm sure) at Rhondda County Girls School, Porth, in South Wales in the 1960s and is the mnemonic for the six towns that make up Stoke-upon-Trent in Staffordshire. If this comes in useful you must be taking part in a pub quiz in the Potteries.

Tunstall, Burslem, Hanley, Stoke, Fenton, Longton

The counties of Northern Ireland

FAT LAD

Fermanagh, Antrim, Tyrone, Londonderry, Armagh, Down

CHAPTER 9

The Weather

Red sky at night –
Shepherds' delight.

Red sky in the morning –
Shepherds' warning.

The American version has sailors instead of shepherds, both occupations having good reason to keep a close eye on the weather.

There are a number of old wives' tales relating to the weather but this is really an ancient wives' tale that was passed on by word of mouth for centuries.

The first written reference, in Middle English, to the phenomenon is in the Wycliffe Bible of 1384 and it appears thus in the 1611 King James Authorised Version of the Bible in the Gospel according to St Matthew, Chapter 16: v 2 – 3:

[Jesus said unto the Pharisees and the Sadducees]

139

When it is evening, ye say, It will be fair weather: for the sky is red.

And in the morning, It will be foul weather to day: for the sky is red and lowring.

Shakespeare noted the phenomenon in his epic poem Venus and Adonis (1593):

Like a red morn that ever yet betokened,

Wreck to the seamen, tempest to the field,

Sorrow to the shepherds, woe unto the birds,

Gusts and foul flaws to herdmen and to herds.

This is more than an ancient wives' tale, being soundly based on science. The sky is full of dust particles and water droplets that scatter the sun's rays. During the day when the sun is high, the sunlight has to pass through less atmosphere before we see it. The sunlight is scattered more effectively by short wavelengths – which is why the sky is blue.

At sunset, when the sun is low on the horizon, the sunlight has to pass through more atmosphere than when the sun is overhead. The shorter wavelengths are filtered out, leaving only the longer wavelengths of red, orange and yellow light for us to see. As the sun sets in the west and our weather generally comes in from the west, if there are no clouds in the sky, there is a good chance of clear skies and fine weather ahead.

In the morning, equally, the sun rising in the east has to pass through more atmosphere, and when it reflects the water vapour and dust particles of a weather system that has come in from the west, it will be coloured reddish. A red sky in the morning means that there is a high water content in the atmosphere – and rain is probably on the way.

St Swithin's Day

St Swithin's Day, if thou dost rain,

Full forty days it will remain.

St Swithin's Day, if thou be fair,

For forty days, 'twill rain na mair.

St Swithin (properly Swithun), was Bishop of Winchester in the 9th Century and requested to be buried in humble surroundings outside the cathedral so the sweet rain of heaven could fall on him. More than one hundred years later, the monks decided that this was not a fitting resting place for him and arranged to move his remains to a shrine inside the cathedral on July 15, 971.

According to legend, there was a great storm that day and then torrential rain for forty days. Believing that this was evidence of St Swithin weeping in despair, the monks decided against moving his remains. This led to the old wives' tale that if it rained on July 15, it would rain continuously for 40 days. And vice versa.

There is some meteorological basis for this: by the middle of July, the weather systems – particularly the position of the jetstream – seem pretty settled and will carry on for another six weeks. If the jetstream settles to the south of Britain, cold and wet weather comes in from the north; if it settles to the north, continental high pressure allows warm and dry weather to come in from the south.

The French have a similar 40-day rhyme on July 19, St Gervais Day:

Quand il pleut à la St Gervais,
il pleut quarante jours après.

July 15 is The One Day in the book and film One Day. Why the author David Nicholls chose St Swithin's Day as The One Day to be revisited by two university friends every year for 20 years is not clear, although he does acknowledge owing a debt to Billy Bragg for his song St Swithin's Day.

St Dunstan's Day

Last frosts before summer:

Another old wives' tale involving the weather and a bishop and a saint – in this case St Dunstan. Before he became Bishop of Worcester, and subsequently Archbishop of Canterbury (960 – 978), he set himself up as a brewer in the days when there was much competition between ale producers and cider makers.

A sequence of frost-free springs in Somerset had been a boon for the cider makers. In the face of this he is supposed to have sold his soul to the devil in return for regular May frosts which would kill off the apple blossom, and thus help to kill off the competition to his brewing business. Satan, apparently, agreed to engineer frosts each year between May 17 and May 19, the last being St Dunstan's Day.

To this day, it is not uncommon for the last frosts before summer in lowland southern England to be around these dates.

Oak and Ash

If the oak before the ash,

Then we'll only have a splash.

If the ash before the oak,

Then we'll surely get a soak

This weather folklore, based on when trees come into leaf, may soon become obsolete on two counts. Warmer springs are advancing the oak more quickly than the ash. The Woodland Trust reported in 2008 that the ash had come into leaf before the oak only four times since 1964. And in 2012, it was reported that Ash Dieback Disease, caused by a deadly fungus Chalara fraxinea, posed a very serious threat to the future of almost every ash tree in Britain.

Wind

You always know the way they go

Because they blow from High to Low.

Wind blows from High Pressure to Low Pressure.

Warning of rain

Swallows high, staying dry.

Swallows low, wet 'twill blow.

It appears that as the weather clears after rain, the insects the swallows feed on, dry out their wings better by flying higher. So the swallows fly high to catch them. The insects are also carried higher by the warmer air currents that accompany the dry weather.

And if it is raining or threatening rain, they stay low.

Predicting the harvest

Mist in May, heat in June

Make the harvest come on soon.

General gardening advice

Grow apples for yourself

And pears for your heirs.

Apple trees are much faster growing that pear trees.

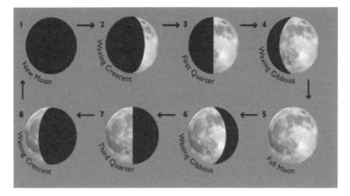

The Phases of the Moon

The Phases of the Moon (the changing shape of what we can see of the Moon) are produced by the alignment of the Earth, the Moon and the Sun. They form a cycle as the Moon orbits the Earth, starting with **1** the New Moon (0% visible), **2** Waxing Crescent (shaped like a capital D), **3** First Quarter (50% visible) and **4** Waxing Gibbous. This part of the cycle takes around 14.77 days

The cycle continues with **5** the Full Moon (100% visible), **6** Waning Gibbous, **7** Third Quarter (50% visible) and **8** Waning Crescent (shaped like a capital C) and back to the start of the cycle again with **1** the New Moon. The whole cycle – a lunar month – takes 29 days 12 hours 43 minutes.

Crescent Moon: less than half is lit.
Gibbous Moon: more than half is lit (from Latin meaning hump-backed).

The mnemonic (in the northern hemisphere) is:
When the moon looks like a capital D, it is not Departing; it is Coming (getting bigger).
When the moon looks like a capital C, it is not Coming; it is Departing (getting smaller).

Temperature

(Celsius and Fahrenheit)

> 30°C is hot, 20 is nice,
>
> 10 is cold, and 0 is ice.

For those of us who still struggle with °C.

Freezing is 0 Celsius, 32 Fahrenheit.

Remember 10°Celsius is 50°Fahrenheit.

Two easy ones to flip: 16°C is 61°F : 28°C is 82°F.

1966 – The unforgettable annus mirabilis for England: the year we won the World Cup. 19°C is 66°F.

20°C is 68°F.

●Converting Fahrenheit to Celsius:

Subtract 32 from the °F and then multiply by 5/9.

Eg: 72°F

72 minus 32 = 40 divided by 5/9 = 22°C

●Converting Celsius to Fahrenheit:

Multiply the °C by 9/5 and then add 32.

Eg: 20°C

20 times 9/5 = 36. Add 32 = 68°F

CHAPTER 10

Time

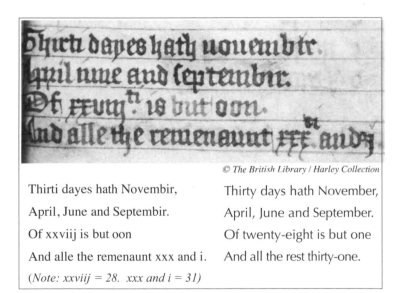

© The British Library / Harley Collection

Thirti dayes hath Novembir,
April, June and Septembir.
Of xxviij is but oon
And alle the remenaunt xxx and i.
(*Note: xxviij = 28. xxx and i = 31*)

Thirty days hath November,
April, June and September.
Of twenty-eight is but one
And all the rest thirty-one.

It is one of the most popular and oft-repeated rhymes in the English language –Thirty Days Hath September, April, June and November – and has helped countless generations remember the number of days in each month. While researching this book, I discovered this famous rhyme in an early-15th century manuscript in the Harley Collection at the British Library in London. It appears to be the oldest-known written reference to the mnemonic, and is a rare entry in English in the 200-page illuminated Latin codex of religious calendars and prayers.

The commentary in the British Library states that the four-line entry is in the same (quite beautiful) hand as the rest of the first section of the tiny (110mm x 65mm) red leather-bound codex. The written verse dates from around 1425, and is at the bottom of a page on the saints' days for February in a collection of religious calendars.

This is a popular modern-day version:

> Thirty days hath September,
>
> April, June and November.
>
> All the rest have thirty-one.
>
> Except for February alone,
>
> Which hath twenty-eight days clear
>
> And twenty-nine in each Leap year.

When or why November and September changed places in the rhyme is not known (it doesn't make any real difference), but a handwritten entry dated pre-1574 in the Mostyn Papers held at the National Library of Wales, Aberystwyth, has: Thirty Days hath September, April, June and November. February hath twenty-eight and all the rest hath thirty-one.

Groucho Marx may have identified one of the reasons for the popularity and longevity of the rhyme when he said: 'My favourite poem is the one that starts Thirty Days Hath September, because it actually tells you something.'

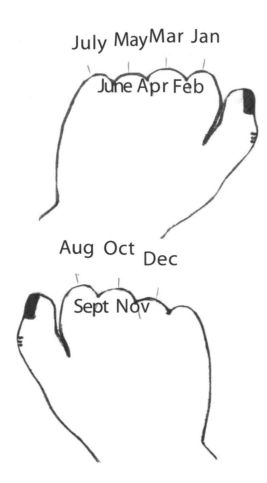

July MayMar Jan

June Apr Feb

Aug Oct Dec

Sept Nov

A visual way of remembering the days of the months. Make a fist. Start on the first knuckle and go across the knuckles and spaces in between. A knuckle is 31 days, a dip is 30. After July, go on to the first knuckle on the other hand, which is August. February is 28 or 29.

Spring Forward, Fall Back

This is the fail-safe for remembering whether the clocks go forward or back in the spring and autumn (the Fall).

They Spring forward in Spring (on the last Sunday in March) and Fall back in the Autumn (on the last Sunday in October).

Despite this simple mnemonic, it is surprising how many people don't know which way the clocks change.

In March, the clocks change at 01.00 Greenwich Mean Time (because we're on GMT then) and at 02.00 British Summer Time in October (because we're on BST then).

There has been some support recently for moves to change the system, effectively by losing an hour of daylight in the mornings and gaining an hour of daylight in the evenings.

It works like this. In the autumn, when the clocks would normally fall back to GMT, there would be no change. So we would still be on BST, which is GMT+1. In the spring, the clocks would go forward as normal, and this would be to Double BST (BST+1 or GMT +2).When it came to the autumn again, the clocks would go back an hour, again to GMT +1 (or BST).

There's nothing miraculous about this – it's not creating more daylight. What it is doing is using the daylight we get in a more effective and efficient way.

This simply would be the singular, most happiness-inducing leglislation that any government could introduce – so it's not going to happen.

Apart from the sheer enjoyment of having an extra hour of daylight/sunlight in the evenings, there are a number of other real and important benefits. According to the Transport Research Laboratory, it could prevent around 100 deaths and 450 serious injuries on the roads by decreasing the amount of driving in the dark. The NHS would save £138m annually by the reduction in motoring accidents.

Because the evenings would be lighter, the surge in energy demand as people turn on lights and heating when they arrive home between 4pm and 6pm would be lowered. A study at Cambridge University found the change could save 5% of the nation's electricity and reduce carbon dioxide emissions by an estimated one million tons a year.

Darker evenings mean that crime, especially burglary, muggings and vandalism, goes up. The London Chamber of Commerce believes that millions of pounds could be saved by Britain coming into line with Western European time.

An extra hour of daylight in the evening would be a boon for outdoor sports activities. The Football Association, the England and Wales Cricket Board and the Lawn Tennis Association all back the move, saying the extra hour of daylight in the evening would offer greater opportunities for extra participation.

It would be an important boost too for the tourism industry because attractions (eg Alton Towers) could extend their opening hours (especially in spring and autumn). And it would also benefit the Scottish ski-ing industry. One estimate has said it could boost the hospitality and tourist industry by £4bn and could create 80,000 jobs. Sticking points in the past have been farmers and people in Scotland, but campaigners for change say opposition on those fronts is falling away.

As the climate change campaigners 10:10 said: 'It would make us happier, healthier and better off'.

The Four Seasons

Their start dates are always twentysomething: count the vowels in the season's name for the number.

Spring   (1 vowel)   21 March

Summer   (2 vowels)   22 June

Autumn   (3 vowels)   23 September

Winter   (2 vowels)   22 December

These dates roughly correspond with the spring and autumn equinoxes, and the summer and winter solstices, which approximately fall on the 21st day of the last month of every quarter.

The equinox is when the sun is directly above the equator, and so the length of day and night are approximately the same.

The solstice is when the tilt of the earth's axis is directly towards and away from the sun, giving us the longest and shortest days of the year.

The Quarter Days

These roughly coincide with the equinoxes and solstices, each representing a quarter of the year – spring, summer, autumn and winter. The mnemonic is: the number of letters in the month denotes the second digit in the twentysomething number. Christmas is the exception, most people knowing what day it falls on.

March	(5 letters)	25	Lady Day
June	(4 letters)	24	Midsummer Day
September	(9 letters)	29	Michaelmas Day
December		25	Christmas Day

The four Quarter Days were part of a list of special days in the Christian Calendar, when among other things, rents and leases were due, taxes were collected and work contracts started and ended. By tradition, the rent for British allotments is due on Michaelmas Day.

If you have ever wondered why the British tax year ends on April 5 (give or take a day) – blame it on the Quarter Days. When Britain eventually moved to the Gregorian Calendar in 1752, a number of days had to be lost because the old Julian Calendar had calculated that the year was 11 minutes longer than it actually was.

Over a long time, this added up to a long time, and so it was decreed that 11 days had to be lost. Previously, Lady Day, March 25, had been the end of the financial year, but businessmen in the City protested about the changes and were granted an extra 11 days to settle their affairs. That's why April 5 is the end of the tax year.

Signs of the Zodiac

A Tense Grey Cat Lay Very Low,
Sneaking Slowly, Contemplating A Paw

Aries, Taurus, Gemini, Cancer, Leo, Virgo, Libra,
Scorpio, Sagittarius, Capricorn, Aquarius, Pisces.

This verse is by English preacher and poet Isaac Watts
(1674 -1748), who wrote more than 700 hymns.

The Ram, the Bull, the heavenly Twins,

And next the Crab, the Lion shines,

The Virgin and the Scales,

The Scorpion, Archer and Sea-Goat,

The Man who pours the water out,

And Fish with glittering tails.

CHAPTER 11

The Sciences

The speed of light

We guarantee certainty, clearly referring to this light mnemonic

The number of letters in each word gives the answer.

299,792,458 metres per second

Temperature of Absolute Zero

An Iceberg Yes! I Froze

Minus 273.15° Celsius

Soon Chill Overtakes People Totally

Minus 459.67° Fahrenheit

The Periodic Table

A table listing the chemical elements in terms of increasing atomic number which was formalised by the Russian scientist Dmitri Mendeleyev in 1869.

Elements 1 - 10

Hell, Here Little Beatniks Brandish
Countless Numbers Of Flick kNivEs

H, He, L, Be, B, C, N, O, F, Ne

Hydrogen, Helium, Lithium, Beryllium, Boron, Carbon, Nitrogen, Oxygen, Fluorine, Neon.

Elements 11 - 18

Naughty Maggie Always Sips
Pure Sweet Claret

Na Mg Al Si P S Cl

Sodium, Magnesium, Aluminium, Silicon, Phosphorus, Sulphur, Chlorine.

These two short periods can also be remembered by simple abbreviations.

1 – 10: Hhelibeb can of nee

11 – 17: Namgal sips claret

There are at present 118 elements in the Periodic Table, Element 117, Ununseptium, symbols Uus, has not yet been discovered.

The order of the Earth's atmospheres

The Strong Man's Triceps Explode

Troposphere, Stratosphere, Mesosphere, Thermosphere, Exosphere.

The electromagnetic spectrum

(From the shortest waves to the longest: the shorter the wave, the higher the energy).

Cary Grant eXpects Unanimous Votes In Movie Reviews Tonight

Cosmic rays

Gamma rays

X-rays

Ultra violet light

Visible light

Infrared

Microwaves

Radio waves

Television

The Mohs Scale of Hardness for Minerals

Those Girls Can Flirt And Other Queer Things Can Do

1 Talc	6 Orthoclase (feldspar)
2 Gypsum	7 Quartz
3 Calcite	8 Topaz
4 Fluorite	9 Corundum
5 Apatite	10 Diamond

The first two can be scratched by a thumbnail. The next four can be scratched by a penknife and the last four will scratch glass. A fingernail has a hardness of 2.5: a 2p piece has a hardness of 5.5. Each mineral can scratch another with a lower Mohs number.

I assumed Mohs was an acronym for Measure of Hardness Scale. In fact Herr Friederich Mohs was born in 1773 with this presciently appropriate surname: he became a German minerologist of note and gave his name to the scale which he codified around 1800 and which is still in use today.

Geological time periods

Camels Often Sit Down Carefully.

Perhaps Their Joints Creak?

Persistent Early Oiling Might Prevent

Permanent Rheumatism

Cambrian, Ordovician, Silurian, Devonian, Carboniferous,

Permian, Triassic, Jurassic, Cretaceous,

Palaeocene, Eocene, Oligocene, Miocene, Pliocene,

Pleistocene, Recent (Holocene).

Order of the biological groupings in taxonomy

King Philip Came Over For Good Sex

Keep Ponds Clean Or Fish Get Sick

Kingdom, Phylum, Class, Order,
Family, Genus, Species

The five classes of vertebrate animals

FARM-B:

Fish, Amphibians, Reptiles, Mammals, Birds.

The first three are cold-blooded, the last two warm-blooded.

Nerves:

Cranial

On Old Olympus's Towering Tops,
A Finn and German Viewed Some Hops

Olfactory, optic, oculomotor, trochlear, trigeminal, abducent, facial, auditory, glossopharyngeal, vagus, spinal accessory, hypoglossal.

Branches of facial nerve

Two Zebras Bought My Car

Temporal, Zygomatic, Buccal, Mandibular, Cervical.

Superior orbital tissue of skull

The order of nerves that pass through the superior orbital tissue in the skull. This is included solely for the mnemonic, not the subject matter.

Lazy French Tarts Lie
Naked In Anticipation

Lacrimal, Frontal, Trochlear, Lateral,

Nasociliary, Internal, Abducent.

Course of the Lingual Nerve

(Which takes a convoluted route around the tongue)

The Lingual Nerve

Took a curve

Around the Hyoglossus.

'Well I'll be f****d,'

Said Wharton's Duct,

The b*****d's gone and crossed us.

Bones:

Spinal Column

Clever Tom Looks Silly Clot

Cervical, Thoracic, Lumbar, Sacrum, Coccyx.

Arm

Some Crooks Have Underestimated Royal Canadian Mounted Police

Scapula, Clavicle, Humerus, Ulna,

Radius, Carpals, Metacarpals, Phalanges.

Leg

Help Five Police To Find Ten Missing Prisoners

Hip, Femur, Patella, Tibia, Fibula, Tarsals, Metatarsals, Phalanges.

The wrist (carpals)

Some Lovers Try Positions That They Can't Handle

Scaphoid, Lunate, Triquetrum, Pisiform, Trapezium, Trapezoid, Capitate, Hamate.

The skull

Old People From Texas Eat Spiders

Occipital, Parietal, Frontal, Temporal, Ethmoid, Sphenoid.

Bones within the ear

HAS

Hammer, Anvil, Stirrup

The three main insect body parts

HAT

Head, Abdomen, Thorax

Major characteristics of living organisms

Newmarket Runs Every
Great Race in May

Nutrition
Respiration
Excretion
Growth
Reproduction
Irritability
Movement

Newmarket considers itself both as the birthplace and the global centre of thoroughbred horses. It is the largest racehorse training centre in Britain and is the home of the first two classic horseraces in Britain, the 1,000 Guineas and the 2,000 Guineas held in May.

Optics

The additive and subtractive mixtures of colours:

Better Get Ready While
Your Mistress Comes Back

Blue + Green + Red = White (additive)

Yellow + Magenta + Cyan = Black (subtractive)

For the oscillation of a pendulum

The wonders of Nature, quoth he

Are always a marvel to me:

That each tick and a tock

of a grandfather clock

$$\text{is } \frac{2\pi\sqrt{l}}{g}$$

Where T = period of the pendulum

l = the length of the pendulum

g = acceleration due to gravity.

The APGAR Score

Devised in 1952 by Canadian paediatrician Dr Virginia Apgar as a simple method to assess quickly the health of babies immediately after childbirth.

Appearance (skin colour)

Pulse

Grimace (reflex irritability)

Activity (muscle tone)

Respiration

There are two marks in each category, and so a perfectly healthy new-born baby will get a score of 10. Strangely, the APGAR score also works in French, German and Spanish.

This is an example of a backronym (See p203).

Resistor colour codes

Electronic resistors have coloured bands on them to denote their level of resistance. The standard colour code is:

Black, Brown, Red, Orange, Yellow, Green, Blue, Violet, Grey, White.

Bad Boys Rough Our Young Girls, But Violet Goes Willingly

Better Be Ready, Or Your Great Big Venture Goes West

(From an old Boy Scout book on electricity).

Bye Bye, Rosie. Off You Go: Birmingham via Great Western

True direction

For converting compass headings back to true ones:

Cadbury's Dairy Milk Very Tasty

Course + Deviation = Magnetic + Variation = True

(Taught at Air Navigation School, RAF Cottesmore, in 1942).

For converting true directions to compass readings:

True Virgins Make Dull Company

True + Variation = Magnetic + Deviation = Compass

Ohm's Law

Virgins Are Rare

Volts = Amps x Resistance

Acid tests

May her rest be long and placid

She added water to the acid.

The other girl did what she oughta

She added acid to the water.

Johnny was a scientist, Johnny is no more.

For what he thought was H_2O was H_2SO_4

Sulphuric acid (H_2SO_4) must be poured into water.
The other way round is dangerous and could prove
fatal. H_2SO_4 certainly should not be drunk.

The Redox Process

Oil Rig

Oxidation is Loss

Reduction is Gain

CHAPTER 12

Astronomy

The Harvard Spectral Classification of Stars

(Stars in descending order of surface temperature).

O B A F G K M.RNS

Oh Be A Fine Girl, Kiss Me
Right Now, Sweetie

Originally the scheme used capital letters running alphabetically, but was later reordered to reflect the surface temperatures. The stars are classified into different types, – O, B, A etc – where each star type is cooler than the previous. O-type stars are blue and hot (c 35,000C) and shine with the power of one million times the Sun's output. Our Sun is classified as a G star.

R,N and S-type stars are cooler but can be added to the classification as can L and T stars, which are brown dwarfs.

O B A F G K M.LT

Officially, Bill Always Felt Guilty
Kissing Monica Lewinsky Tenderly

Henry Norris Russell, the leading theoretical American astronomer of his time, is credited with the original mnemonic, which must have upset many thousands of female students through the years. The alternative is:

Oh Be A Fine Girl,
Kiss Me Right Now...Smack

The five brightest stars

Sirius, Canopus, Alpha Centauri, Arcturus,Vega.

Some Constellations
Actually Aid Vegans

Sirius is twice as bright as any other star in the sky. It is part of the Canis Major constellation and is sometimes called the Dog Star. In ancient Greek times, the dawn rising of Sirius marked the hottest part of the summer, and is thought to be the origin of the phrase the dog days of summer. Alpha Centauri is a binary star system and is visible only in the southern hemisphere.

Order of the Planets

Mercury, Venus, Earth, Mars,
Jupiter, Saturn, Uranus, Neptune, Pluto.

My Very Easy Method.
Just Set Up Nine Planets

Pluto was demoted from full planetary status in 2006.
An American website held a competition for the best
new mnemonic, and the winner was:

My! Very Educated Morons Just
Screwed Up Numerous Planetariums

Other new ones without Pluto are:

My Very Easy Method: Just SUN

My Very Eager Mother Just
Served Up Nibbles

Pluto was discovered in 1930 by Percival Lowell – Pl
– and this doleful mnemonic was written for him. A
favourite:

My Vision, Erased. Mercy! Just
Some Underachiever Now

Distance of the Planets from the Sun

In the following scale, £1 equals one astronomical unit, ie the mean distance from the Earth to the Sun, about 93 million miles.

Mercury	£0.39
Venus	£0.72
Earth	£1.00
Mars	£1.50
Jupiter	£5.20
Saturn	£9.50
Uranus	£19.00
Neptune	£30.00

Size of Planets

Sun – J – SUN

Sun, Jupiter, Saturn, Uranus, Neptune.

The different orders of size (diameter, measured in thousands of miles) are: 865, 89, 75, 32, 31. The Earth comes it at 8 (thousand miles in diameter).

CHAPTER 13

Religion

Books in the Bible

Old Testament:

3 letters and **9** letters gives **39**

New Testament:

3 letters times **9** gives **27**

The Twelve Disciples

This is the way the Disciples run.

Peter, Andrew, James and John,

Phillip and Bartholomew,

Thomas next and Matthew, too,

James the less and Judas the greater,

Simon the Zealot and Judas the traitor.

The Four Gospels

Matthew, Mark, Luke and John,
Went to bed with their trousers on

Don't ask me, but I must have been five or six years old when I first learned this. For some reason it is a memorable couplet.

Why they went to bed with their trousers on I do not know. And come to think of it, they probably didn't wear trousers anyway.

The Ten Commandments

One idle damn Sunday, Dad killed cheating thief and lied to cover it

No other Gods, no idols, don't blaspheme, rest on the Sabbath, respect your parents, don't kill, don't commit adultery, don't steal, don't bear false witness and don't covet.

The Four Horsemen of the Apocalypse

From the Book of Revelation: Chapter 6: v 1-8

What Fool Picks Death?

War, Famine, Pestilence, Death.

The Ten Plagues of Egypt

Exodus: Chapters 7 to 12.

God inflicted these sequential horrors after Pharaoh refused to let Moses lead the Israelites out of Egypt to freedom. It was only when God sent a plague in which all the first-born, man and beast, died (with the Israelites completely untouched) that Pharaoh allowed the children of Israel, 600,000 of them, to leave.

Blood, Frogs, Lice, Pestilence, Flies,
Boils, Hail, Locusts, Darkness, First-born.

Beware Finding Licky Pesty Flies
Beware Handling Licky Dragon Flies

The Seven Deadly Sins

PALE GAS

Pride, Avarice, Lust, Envy, Gluttony, Anger, Sloth.

WASPLEG

Wrath, Avarice, Sloth, Pride, Lust, Envy, Gluttony.

Waspleg is the title of an excellent American book of mnemonics by Bart Benne published in 1988.

The Seven Deadly Sins are not referred to in a cohesive manner in the Bible, but have been a central feature of Catholicism for centuries, Pope Gregory the Great having codified them in the 6th Century.

CHAPTER 14

Music

Guido of Arezzo (991–1050) is regarded as the father of modern musical notation: his solfeggio system became the forerunner of the Do-Re-Mi scale.

The Do-Re-Mi song from the Rodgers and Hammerstein musical and subsequent film The Sound of Music is a brilliant mnemonic for the eight notes in an octave.

Do, Re, Mi, Fa, So, La, Ti, Do

Doe, a deer, a female deer,

Ray, a drop of golden sun,

Me, a name I call myself,

Far, a long long way to run,

Sew, a needle pulling thread,

La, a note to follow so,

Tea, a drink with jam and bread

And that will bring us back to Doe.

Douglas Adams, the author of The Hitchhikers' Guide to the Galaxy, argued that Hammerstein put in the La line – A note to follow So – merely as a placeholder – he couldn't think of anything better or memorable, and so put that line in as a temporary measure meaning to go back to it sometime to improve it. He never did. Adams does have a point – all the other lines have a simple, wonderful beauty about them, except that one.

In an episode of the Simpsons, Homer crashes his car into the statue of a deer, whereupon he shouts 'D'oh', followed by Lisa, 'A deer' and Marge, 'A female deer'.

Notes: (In ascending order)

On the lines of the treble clef

EGBDF

Every Good Boy Deserves Favour

In the spaces of the treble clef

FACE

On the lines of the bass clef

GBDFA

Good Boys Deserve Fruit Always

Grizzly Bears Don't Fly Aeroplanes

ACEG

All Cows Eat Grass

Progression:

Of sharps for sharp key signatures

FCGDAEB

Father Charles Goes Down

And Ends Battle

One sharp, F, denotes the key of G. Two sharps, F and C, denote the key of D. Three sharps, F, C and G, denote the key of A, and so on.

The designated key is one semi-tone above the last sharp on the key signature.

Of flats for flat key signatures

BEADGCF

Battle Ends And Down Goes
Charles's Father

Tuning a guitar

EADGBE: (from the lowest string).

Every Able Dad Goes Bald Eventually

Elephants And Donkeys Grow Big Ears

Four sections of an orchestra:

Stringers Would Be Persecuted

Strings, Woodwind, Brass, Percussion.

Choral Voices:

STAB

Singers Take A Break

Soprano, Tenor, Alto, Bass.

Musical Modes:

I Don't Play Ludo Much After Lessons

Ionian, Dorian, Phrygian, Lydian, Mixolydian, Aeolian, Locrian.

The modes are scales dating from ancient Greece based on what became the white notes on the piano. The Ionian mode goes from C to C (the C major scale). The Dorian mode goes from E to E, and the Aeolian mode goes from A to A in the key of A minor.

CHAPTER 15

Things American

In fourteen hundred and ninety two,
Columbus sailed the ocean blue,
And found this land, land of the Free,
Beloved by you, beloved by me.

This is the start of a poem by Winifred Sackville Stoner junior (1902-1983) called The History of the US.

It goes on

Year seventeen hundred seventy six,
July the Fourth, this date please fix
Within your minds, my children dear,
For that was Independence Year.

The Original 13 States

My Nice New Car Needs Re-Painting.
Maybe Dark Violet? No, Shiny Gold

Massachusetts	Maryland
New Hampshire	Delaware
New York	Virginia
Connecticut	North Carolina
New Jersey	South Carolina
Rhode Island	Georgia
Pennsylvania	

Mount Rushmore

Washington, Jefferson, Lincoln, Roosevelt.

We Just Like Rushmore

The four US presidents carved into a rock face of Mount Rushmore, South Dakota. The heads are 18 metres high.

US Presidents to 1849:

Washington's Army Journeyed Many Miles
And Just Battled Hard To Philadelphia

Washington, George	1789 – 1797
Adams, John	1797 – 1801
Jefferson, Thomas	1801 – 1809
Madison, James	1809 – 1817
Monroe, James	1817 – 1825
Adams, John Quincy	1825 – 1829
Jackson, Andrew	1829 – 1837
Buren, Martin van	1837 – 1841
Harrison, William Henry	1841
Tyler, John	1841 – 1845
Polk, James Knox	1845 – 1849

US Presidents 1849 – 1901:

To Find Pretty British Ladies,
Johnson Gave Him Good Advice:
Check Haagen-Dazs, Check Macy's

Taylor, Zachary	1849 – 1850
Fillmore, Millard	1850 – 1853
Pierce, Franklin	1853 – 1857
Buchanan, James	1857 – 1861
Lincoln, Abraham	1861 – 1865
Johnson, Andrew	1865 – 1869
Grant, Ulysses Simpson	1869 – 1877
Hayes, Rutherford Birchard	1877 – 1881
Garfield, James Abram	1881
Arthur, Chester Alan	1881 – 1885
Cleveland, Grover	1885 – 1889
Harrison, Benjamin	1889 – 1893
Cleveland, Grover	1893 – 1897
McKinley, William	1897 – 1901

US Presidents 1900 – 1945:

Roo Took What He Could Home, Right?

Roosevelt, Theodore	1901 – 1909
Taft, William Howard	1909 – 1913
Wilson, Woodrow	1913 – 1921
Harding, Warren Gamaliel	1921 – 1923
Coolidge, Calvin	1923 – 1929
Hoover, Herbert Clark	1929 – 1933
Roosevelt, Franklin Delano	1933 – 1945

US Presidents 1945 onwards:

The Engineer Knew John Nixon's Ford
Could Really Be Clinton's Blue Oldsmobile

Truman, Harry S.	1945 – 1953
Eisenhower, Dwight David	1953 – 1961
Kennedy, John Fitzgerald	1961 – 1963
Johnson, Lyndon Baines	1963 – 1969
Nixon, Richard Milhouse	1969 – 1974
Ford, Gerald	1974 – 1977
Carter, James Earl	1977 – 1981
Reagan, Ronald	1981 – 1989
Bush, George Herbert Walker	1989 – 1993
Clinton, William Jefferson	1993 – 2001
Bush, George Walker	2001 – 2009
Obama, Barack	2009 –

Ten largest states:

Al Texted Cally: MnMs Are
Never Coloured Orange. Why?

Alaska	Arizona
Texas	Nevada
California	Colorado
Montana	Oregon
New Mexico	Wyoming

Five smallest American states:

Rhodri's Delivered Connie's
New Jersey Near Hampton

Rhode Island, Delaware, Connecticut,

New Jersey, New Hampshire

Ivy League universities:

Your Data Base Contains Pretty Preppy Historic Colleges

Yale, Dartmouth, Brown, Cornell, Princeton,
Penn (University of Pennsylvania), Harvard, Columbia.

A group of eight long-established, rich and prestigious colleges in the north east of the US. Ivy because of ivy-clad walls and League after intercollegiate football games were formalised into an official competition.

The Ivy League has been closely connected with the acronym WASP – White Anglo-Saxon Protestant – a representative of a powerful group that formed the social and political elite in the US and who were generally educated at an Ivy League college.

All American presidents have been male WASPs with the exception of President John Kennedy, who was a (very rich) Roman Catholic – a WASC if you want. And of course, Barack Obama, who rather broke the mould. But he did go to Harvard Law School.

CHAPTER 16

Acronyms & Abbreviations

Medical Notes:

About ten years ago there was a spate of newspaper stories about abbreviations, most of them in bad taste, that doctors were putting on patients' notes.

TATT

Tired All The Time

TEETH

Tried Everything Else, Try Homeopathy

WOT

Waste Of Time

LOBNH

Lights On But Nobody Home

CKBNDY

Completely Knackered, But Not Dead Yet

FLK

Funny Looking Kid

GLM

Good Looking Mum

ARSD

Alcohol Related Sudden Death

UBI

Unexplained Beer Injury

GPO

Good for Parts Only

GOK

God Only Knows

(quite common, apparently).

TATSP

Thick As Two Short Planks

MAGGOT

Medically Able, Go Get Other Transportation

(on the notes of a patient who requested an ambulance home, but didn't need one)

GOMER

Get Out of My Emergency Room

ART

Assuming Room Temperature (i.e. recently died). Ouch!

There were some regional variations as well:

NFN

Normal For Norfolk

Norfolk people had an undeserved reputation for being, well, thick.

NFA

Normal For Andover

This was from the hospital at Winchester, which obviously looked down its nose at its Hampshire neighbour.

And finally one that must have sent shivers down the spine of the medical staff.

KSI

Knows Somebody Important

Dr Phil Hammond, the TV doctor, was quoted as saying they had become something of an art form, but eventually they were banned. The UK Central Council for Nursing, Midwifery and Health Visiting was forced to send out 640,000 letters warning medical staff not to use offensive jargon.

Acronyms:

Acronyms are abbreviations that enter into the language as separate words themselves.

SCUBA

Self-Contained Underwater Breathing Apparatus

RADAR

Radio Detection And Ranging

LASER

Light Amplification by Stimulated Emission of Radiation

YUPPIE

Young Urban Professional, popular in the 1980s but out of fashion now. It was ousted by

LOMBARD

Loads Of Money But A Right (fill in your own D-word)

Then the series became more family oriented:

DINKIES

Double Income, No Kids

SITCOM

Single Income, Two Children, Outrageous Mortgage

ORCHID

One Recent Child, Hideously In Debt

People from the computers systems and IT department have been known to leave notes on the back of office chairs. Family members have even been known to use it in reference to me.

PICNIC

Problem In Chair, Not In Computer

And a chauvinist warning that could come in useful in a darkened nightclub;

BOBFOC

Body off Baywatch, Face off Crimewatch

TWIRLY

Am I Too Early?

All people in England over 60 are eligible for free off-peak bus travel, which in most areas is from 9.30am to 11pm. Bus drivers have got very used to the pained question, at around 9.30 in the morning: Am I too early? (to qualify for the free travel concession).

CHUK

An acronymic imperative from London stockbrokers Seymour Pierce to their clients on what to do with Choices UK shares.

DUMP

Destitute Unemployed Mature Professional

HOPEFUL

Hard-up Old Person Expecting Full Useful Life

NIMBY

Not In My Back Yard

Phrase attributed to Tory minister Nicholas Ridley in the 1980s to describe a general attitude against any developments in a local area. See also:

BANANA

Build Absolutely Nothing Anywhere Near Anywhere

CAVE

Citizens Against Virtually Everything

NOPE

Not On Planet Earth

SNAFU

Situation Normal, All Fouled Up (polite version)

NORWICH

Two post-war examples written on the back of envelopes of letters sent home.

Nickers Off Ready When I Come Home

SWALK

Sealed With A Loving Kiss

BIFFO

Big Ignorant Fellah From Offaly (polite version)

I first heard the BIFFO nickname 25 years ago. It was given to a big, blunt Fleet Street newspaper executive from Lancashire and stood for Big Ignorant Fellah From Oldham (also the polite version) The joke was that he thought it was meant as a term of endearment, Biffo being a cuddly anthropomorphic bear in The Beano comic dating back 50 years.

But it may be of Irish origin, because it is used as a fond and occasionally pejorative term for the natives of Offaly, a county in the south of Ireland. The former Prime Minister of the Republic, Brian Cowen, is almost universally known as Biffo.

Not to be confused with BUFFALO

Big Ugly Fellah From Around Laois-Offaly (polite version again). Laois is an adjoining county.

BRICS

Brazil, Russia, India, China, South Africa

Jim O'Neill, global economist at Goldman Sachs, invented the term in 2001 to highlight the economic potential of the four BRIC countries which could eclipse the combined economies of the current richest countries in the world by 2050. The four BRIC countries represent a quarter of the land area of the earth, and 40 per cent of its population. South Africa became the fifth country in 2011.

PIGS

Portugal, Italy, Greece, Spain.

Countries in the southern part of the Eurozone, often described so in terms of their problems with sovereign debt. This acronym caused some acrimony, and was banned by the Financial Times and Barclays.

GOATs

Government Of All the Talents

Name used to describe Gordon Brown's administration from 2007 to 2010. Who said irony was dead?

CHAOS

Can't Have Anyone Over Syndrome

Not inviting people round to your house because it is so messy and untidy.

NEET

Not in Education, Employment or Training

The saddest entry in the book: in 2011, 794,000
19–24 year olds were in this category.

ASBO

Anti-Social Behaviour Order

Introduced by Tony Blair in 1998 to tackle low-level
crime and anti-social behaviour. Generally thought to
be unsuccessful, being scrapped in 2010 by the Tories.

MAMIL

Overheard at cash desk in cycle shop Halfords: 'Serve
the Mamil at Desk Two'.

Middle-Aged Man In Lycra

FILTH

Failed In London, Try Hong Kong

SKI

Spending the Kids' Inheritance

As in 'We are going SKI-ing' – to describe an expensive
holiday in later life (and probably not ski-ing).

In use I am told in Oman as long ago as 1995.

KIPPERS

Kids In Parents' Pockets Eroding Retirement Savings

Adult children, often thirtysomethings, who still live at the parental home. Phenomenon identified by British financial company the Prudential in 2003.

SMIDSY

An acronym used by London taxi-drivers in this fashion: I had another Smidsy today. It means that they were involved in a minor accident and that the other party said 'Sorry mate. I didn't see you.'

CRAFT

A fitting entry for this book, especially for those who experience senior moments.

Can't Remember A Flipping Thing (polite version)

Where should you sit on an aeroplane?

DAWN

Day Aisle, Window Night

Choose an aisle seat during the day so you can stretch your legs and move around a bit. Choose a window seat in the night, so you sleep uninterrupted without people clambering all over you all night.

POSH

Port Out, Starboard Home

There is no evidence that this was ever used on the luxury liners to and from Britain to the colonies in the Far East (the theory is that posh passengers would have been shaded from the sun in both directions), but as acronyms go, it is pretty neat. Rich passengers were meant to have POSH stamped on their tickets, but there does not seem to be any truth in this. The liners were in service from the 1840s on, but it was 1918 before posh was first used to mean smart, exclusive and associated with the upper class.

Here is a weird one. Paul Torday's follow-up book to his bestselling Salmon Fishing In Yemen was The Irresistible Inheritance Of Wilberforce. His hero was so deluded and delusioned that he could only remember what happened to his wife by the mnemonic:

TNMWWTTW

The Night My Wife Went Through The Windscreen

Well I said it was weird.

MOM-G

Although not a mnemonic, a useful secret acronym.

It's Welsh:

Mas o'ma – Gloi:

Get Out Of Here – Quick!

Checklists:

For aircraft:

CIGAR

Controls, Instruments, Gas, Altitude indicator, Radio

For landing:

GUMPS

Gas, Undercarriage, Mixture, Pilot strapped in, Speed

BUMFH

Australian variation of GUMPS

Brakes, Undercarriage, Mixture, Fuel, Hatches and Harnesses.

Starting a long car journey:

PETROL

Petrol, Electrolyte (battery), Tyres, Radiator, Oil, Lights

Survival expert Ray Mears's mnemonic for checking his vehicle was OK before setting out on a journey, which in his case was generally a bit more than popping out to the local shop.

And for motorbikes:

BOLTS

Brakes, Oil, Lights, Tyres, Steering and Suspension

For small children:

Hideous Fools, Morons, Keep Silent!

This is the Nanny's Mnemonic – I'm glad we never had nannies like that. But it's not as bad as it sounds.

It's the checklist for ensuring that their charges are presentable.

Hair brushed?

Face washed?

Middle neat?

Knees clean?

Shoes brushed and tied?

Backronyms

A backronym is a word used as an acronym although not originally intended as one.

The Apgar Test earlier in the book (Page 165) is a backronym, because a doctor named Apgar devised a test for the health of new-born babies, and the five letters in her surname were used to create an acronym. If the doctor had been called Smith, we wouldn't have had an acronym for the test.

The most famous backronym is SOS – Save Our Souls or Save Our Ship. It comes from the Morse Code (see page 223) which was made up of dots and dashes. The code for S was dot dot dot and for O dash dash dash. So dot dot dot dash dash dash dot dot dot became the Morse Code distress signal on account of its sheer simplicity.

The SOS distress signal was first adopted by Germany in 1905 and became the international standard in 1908. The Germans chose the code; it had nothing to do with the letters the code represented. It was only later that the English backronym was attached to the code.

FORD

Another backronym, current some time ago, was for Ford cars:

First On Race Day (if you liked them),
Found On Road Dead
or Fix Or Repair Daily (if you didn't).

Airlines became an easy target at one time for humorous and cutting acronyms.

SABENA

The name of the former Belgian national airline Sabena (Société Anonyme Belge d'Exploitation de la Navigation Aérienne) formed an acronym in French. In English it was transcribed as

Such A Bad Experience, Never Again.

Perhaps there was something in that – the airline went bust in 2001.

ALITALIA

Always Late In Take-off, Always Late In Arrival

Airplane Landed In Tokyo And Luggage In Alaska.

A bit unfair – I have always found the Italian carrier a proud and efficient airline.

QANTAS

Quick And Nasty Transportation, Any Survivors?

Originally an official acronym for Queensland and Northern Territories Aerial Services.

TAP   (Transportes Aéreos Portugueses)

Take A Parachute

The national airline of Portugal didn't have a good name at one time, although in 2011, it was rated the safest airline in Western Europe.

CHAPTER 17

The Life of Pi

Pi deserves its own little section for the sheer volume of mnemonics.

It is the 16th letter of the Greek alphabet and owes its fame to the fact that it is the symbol of the ratio of the circumference of a circle to its diameter – an infinite number 22 over 7. To four decimal places it is 3.1415

Area of a circle

Apple Pies Are Square

$a = \pi r^2$

Circumference of a circle

Cherry Pie Delicious

$c = \pi d$

To measure the area and circumference of a circle, we will use a £1 coin. It is probably the most used circular object in the land – there were 1,474,000,000 of them in circulation in 2010.

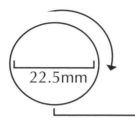

70.7mm

Area of a £1 coin: a = πr²

The radius of a £1 coin is 11.25mm. (Diameter ÷ 2)

11.25² = 126.56 x π = 397.596 sq mm.

Circumference of £1 coin: c = πd

The diameter of a £1 coin is 22.5mm.

π x 22.5 mm = 70.7mm.

The following mnemonics are all based on counting the number of letters in each word of a sentence, or verse, or indeed a very long poem.

To 6 decimal places:

How I wish I could calculate pi

3.141592

To 7 decimal places:

May I have a large container of coffee?

3.1415926

To 14 decimal places:

How I want a drink, alcoholic of course,

After the heavy chapters

Involving quantum mechanics.

3.14159265358979

To 30 decimal places:

(From the Mensa Journal)

Sir, I send a rhyme excelling

In sacred truth and rigid spelling;

Numerical sprites elucidate

All my own striving can't relate

If nature gain

Not you complain

Tho' Dr Johnson fulminate

3.141592653589793238462643383279

For the reciprocal of pi:

Can I remember the reciprocal?

0.318310

Pi certainly brings out something in the scientific world: there are hundreds of websites devoted to the little Greek letter. A number of them give Pi to one million decimal places. In September 2010, it was reported that a Japanese systems engineer had calculated the value of pi to five trillion (5,000,000,000,000) decimal places, breaking the previous record of 2.7 trillion. His computer took 90 days to reach the figure but it did not impress his wife – she pointed out that the project had enormously increased their electricity bill.

On the internet, you can purchase a Pi to a million decimal places poster, 4ft by 8ft. I know it shouldn't, but actually it looks quite cool. In America a number of people celebrate Pi Day on March 14 (3.14) which also happens to be Albert Einstein's birthday. There is also another unofficial holiday called Pi Approximation Day on July 22 (22/7). The celebrations generally involve eating pies.

CHAPTER 18

The Miscellany Box

The G8 countries

The Group of Eight is an informal body made up of the governments of Canada, France, Germany, Italy, Japan, Russia, the United Kingdom and the U.S. The European Union is also represented at meetings.

These eight countries contain about 14 per cent of the world's population yet control more than 55 per cent of the world's economic output.

GUS CUK FRIJ

Germany	France
United States	Russia
Canada	Italy
United Kingdom	Japan

The members of OPEC

The 12 members of the Organisation of Petroleum Exporting Countries control more than two thirds of the world's oil reserves.

EQUI- VALANSKI

Ecuador	Libya
Qatar	Angola
United Arab Emirates	Nigeria
Iraq	Saudi Arabia
Venezuela	Kuwait
Algeria	Iran

This Russian-sounding mnemonic is slightly ironic, because Russia, one of the world's biggest oil producers, is not a member.

Dewey Decimal
Library Classification

The system is made up of ten main categories, each divided into ten sub-categories, each of which is then further divided into ten sub-divisions.

The ten main categories are:

General Phil Reckoned Social Language Should Treat Art Like History

000 – General

100 – Philosophy

200 – Religion

300 – Social Sciences

400 – Languages

500 – Science

600 – Technology

700 – The Arts

800 – Literature

900 – History

The Most Distinguished Order of St Michael and St George

Founded in 1818 by George, Prince Regent, who later became George IV. Originally for the inhabitants of the Ionian Islands and Malta, later for any official in colonial affairs and the foreign and diplomatic service.

There are three classes of the order:

3 Companion of the Order
   of St Michael and St George:

CMG: Call Me God

2 Knight/Dame Commander of the Order
   of St Michael and St George:

KCMG: Kindly Call Me God

1 Knight/Dame Grand Cross of the Order
   of St Michael and St George:

GCMG : God Calls Me God

Lord Baden-Powell, who was awarded the GCMG in 1927, always described recipients of the CMG as Colonial Made Gentlemen.

Order of the British Empire

Established by George V in 1917, the most junior British order of chivalry, and also the largest, with more than 100,000 living members.

There are 8,960 Commanders. There are no limits on the number of Officers and Members, but no more than 858 Officers and 1,464 Members may be appointed each year. Its motto is For God and the Empire.

MOCK-G

MBE

Member of the Order of the British Empire

OBE

Officer of the Order of the British Empire

CBE

Commander of the Order of the British Empire

KBE

Knight/Dame Commander of the Order of the British Empire

GBE

Knight/Dame Grand Cross of the Order of the British Empire

British Titles

Did Marky Ever Visit Barmouth Beach?

Duke, Marquess, Earl, Viscount, Baron, Baronet.

Only sons of dukes and marquesses, and daughters of dukes, marquesses and earls can use their Christian names in their titles. Lady Diana Spencer was correctly named so – she was a lady in her own right, being the daughter of an Earl.

Viscounts and barons use the title Lord and their wives Lady, but never with their Christian name.

For some reason television, and especially the BBC, seems to be the worst culprit in this matter. Hardly a day went by in the coverage of the 2012 Olympic Games in London without a reference to Sebastian Coe as Lord Sebastian Coe. It made me want to throw my running shoes at the TV.

Lord Coe was made a life peer in 2000, and has had a glittering and varied career, being a world-record and Olympic gold medal-winning middle-distance runner, a Conservative MP, the head of the successful bid to hold the Olympics in London in 2012 and then the chairman of the Organising Committee.

He was brought up in Sheffield, South Yorkshire, and I am sure he would never have wanted anyone to think that he was the son of a duke or marquess.

Even the wonderful, inestimable Clare Balding called him Lord Sebastian Coe in one broadcast – Clare with your background, you should know better.

Similarly, Lord Owen is the politician David Owen and is a life peer; not being the son of a duke or marquess, he is never Lord David Owen . His wife, Debbie, is Lady Owen or Debbie Owen, never Lady Debbie Owen.

It is the same for baronets and knights. Sir Mark Thatcher is a baronet and his wife Sarah is therefore Lady Thatcher. The other Lady Thatcher, Sarah's more famous namesake, is usually known these days as Baroness Thatcher, although she was formerly better known when she was Prime Minister as Mrs Thatcher.

Sir Richard Branson can be called Sir Richard or Richard Branson. His wife is Lady Branson or Joan, but never Lady Joan or Lady Joan Branson.

If life peers keep more than one name, they must hyphenate it, which means in House of LordsLand that it becomes one word. When Andrew Lloyd Webber (no hyphen) is lording it, he is called Lord Lloyd-Webber.

The Premier Cru Wines of Bordeaux

Teletubby jabbed by a pencil

(Lala, MMR, HB)

Lala: Chateau Latour (Pauillac)

          Chateau Lafite Rothschild (Pauillac)

MMR: Chateau Margaux (Margaux)

          Chateau Mouton-Rothschild (Pauillac)

HB: Chateau Haut-Brion (Graves)

In 1855 by order of Napoleon III, the wines of the Medoc were classified into five divisions, but of the thousands of wines submitted, only 60 were thought worthy of classification and only four wines were granted premier grand cru status (one of which, Haut-Brion, was not from the Medoc, but from Graves). The classification has remained unchanged since, save that Mouton-Rothschild was admitted to the first rank in 1973.

These are among the best wines in the world, and they are extraordinarily expensive: when I wrote the first edition of this book in 2010, Berry Brothers had a bottle of 1982 Chateau Lafite Rothschild available for £5,250 (inc VAT). I said you had better hurry – there are only three bottles left. Well, they have sold out now.

The most expensive wine held at Averys in Bristol in 2012 was another Lafite Rothschild, this time vintage 2010. Six bottles will set you back £7,453 (plus duty and VAT).

Ant and Dec

Some people who may think this is important find it difficult to tell the two ubiquitous TV presenters apart. They are always together. The Bill Nighy character in Love Actually, who didn't know which was which (or perhaps elided them into one person), addresses them: AntorDec.

Ant (Anthony David McPartlin) is always on the left on TV and in photos. Dec (Declan Joseph Oliver Donnelly) is always on the right on TV and in photos.

This follows the 180 degree rule, which is a basic film-editing principle that two people in the same scene should always have the same left/right relationship to each other. They seem to have taken this rule to the nth degree, as in almost all of their TV appearances, Ant is on the left and Dec on the right. A is before D in the alphabet, so start from left with A.

Ant = Anterior, to the fore, the one with the big fore-head

Dec = Decrease, getting smaller, the smaller one.

The Harry Potter Books:

This is very useful in remembering the names and the order of JK Rowling's series of seven world best-selling books. It comes in handy remembering the films, too.

Please Can Pupils
in Gryffindor
Open Harry's Door?

1 HP and the Philosopher's Stone

2 HP and the Chamber of Secrets

3 HP and the Prisoner of Azkaban

4 HP and the Goblet of Fire

5 HP and the Order of the Phoenix

6 HP and the Half-Blood Prince

7 HP and the Deathly Hallows

The last book was made into a film in two parts.

Creature Collections:

Some of this entry will surely come in useful one day. It is part of a list of 75 compiled by a late colleague Nigel Thomas as an addition to the style-book at The Mail on Sunday.

Apes – shrewdness

Boars – sounder

Capercaillies – tok

Cats – cluster

Crows – murder

Finches – charm

Foxes – skulk

Frogs – army

Goats – trip

Hawks – cast

Herons – siege

Hogs – drift

Jellyfish – smack

Kittens – kindle

Larks – exaltation

Magpies – tiding

Moles – labour

Mules – barren

Nightingales – watch

Peacocks – muster

Ravens – wickedness

Rhinoceroses – crash

Rooks – parliament

Starlings – murmuration

Swans – bevy

Toads – knot

Turtledoves – pitying

Woodcocks – fall

The genre lends itself to some modern-day human examples: a Bevy of Alcoholics; an Attitude of Teenagers; and a Brace of Orthodontists.

A	•– *di-dah*	aLONE	N	–• *dah dit*	NAUGHty
B	–••• *dah-di-di-dit*	BEAUtifully	O	––– *dah-dah-dah*	OUR OLD OAK
C	–•–• *dah-di-dah-dit*	COME a CROPper	P	•––• *di-dah-dah-dit*	PoLITE PERson
D	–•• *dah-di-dit*	DAINtily	Q	––•– *dah-dah-di-dah*	QUITE QUEER and QUAINT
E	• *dit*	Egg	R	•–• *di-dah-dit*	ReWARDing
F	••–• *di-di-dah-dit*	For a FORTnight	S	••• *di-di-dit*	Sh sh sh
G	––• *dah-dah-dit*	GOOD GRACious	T	– *dah*	Tea
H	•••• *di-di-di-dit*	Ha ha ha ha	U	••– *di-di-dah*	underNEATH
I	•• *di-dit*	Is it?	V	•••– *di-di-di-dah*	Very verBOSE
J	•––– *di-dah-dah-dah*	JaPAN'S JAM JARS	W	•–– *di-dah-dah*	WithOUT WASTE
K	–•– *dah-di-dah*	KISS me KATE	X	–••– *di-dah-dah-dit*	ExTRA EXpense
L	•–•• *di-dah-di-dit*	LiNOleum	Y	–•–– *dah-dah-di-dah*	YELLOW yacht's YARN
M	–– *dah-dah*	MY MATE	Z	––•• *dah-dah-di-dit*	ZEB-ZEB ra-ra

The Morse Code:

A binary code for transmitting messages, devised by US inventor Samuel Morse in 1837. Each letter has its own unique combination of dots (short) and dashes (long).

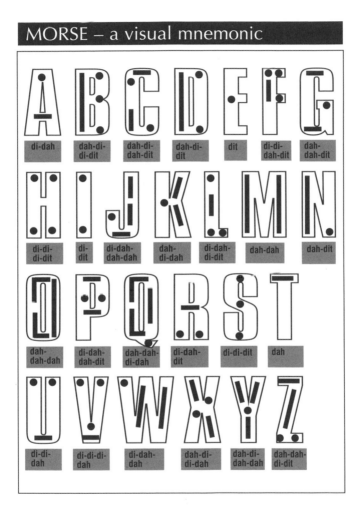

Colours of the Olympic Rings

BY BGR

Blue, Yellow, Black, Green, Red

(in order from left to right)

Records are set BY jumping BiGgeR

The rings were chosen as the symbol of the modern Olympic Games by Baron Pierre de Coubertin in 1913. They represent five continents: North and South America count as one continent, and Antarctica is excluded. Bit harsh on the Antarcticans – they would have done quite well in the Winter Olympics.

No continent is represented by any specific colour.

A trick question in a pub quiz could be: What are Olympic gold medals made of? Answer, Silver, well 92.5 per cent.

Units of Alcohol

The amount of alcohol in drinks is measured in units, one unit in the UK being 10ml by volume or 8g by weight of pure alcohol. People seem to have trouble working out how much alcohol is in a particular drink. It is simple to calculate the amount of units in any drink: think of that nice museum in South Kensington.

V&A = U

Multiply together the Volume of the drink in litres and the Alcohol By Volume of the drink.

So for example, an average glass, 150ml (15cl), of white wine, typically 12% ABV, is 0.150 x 12 = 1.8 units.

A 440ml can of lager, typically 5% ABV, will be 2.2 units, and a pint of beer (568ml, say 3.5%) is 1.98 units.

The Government-recommended daily limit for men is 3 to 4 units a day, and 2 to 3 units a day for women.

The Seven Dwarfs

This was Walt Disney's first animated feature film, released in 1937, and despite his wife Lillian saying 'No one's ever going to pay a dime to see a dwarf picture,' it has become one of the most loved and successful films ever. The Seven Dwarfs were named

Dopey, Doc, Grumpy, Sneezy,
Sleepy, Happy and Bashful

In 2010 in the Houses of Parliament car park, a junior minister's driver reversed into the Daimler of John Bercow, the Speaker of the House of Commons. Mr Bercow, a diminutive figure, quickly appeared and told the Lib Dem MP Simon Burns: 'I'm not Happy.'

To which Mr Burns replied, quick as a flash: 'OK, so which one of the Seven Dwarfs are you then?'

It appears that Mr Bercow is not the most popular member of the House of Commons; a Conservative, but his fellow Tories hated him which is why the Labour party voted him in as Speaker in 2010. So here's a mnemonic for the Seven Dwarfs paying homage to Mr Bercow.

Daimler Dented!
Grumpy Speaker
Says His Bit

Dopey, Doc, Grumpy, Sneezy, Sleepy, Happy, Bashful

The Spleen

You don't often get spleen and beautiful in the same sentence. So how about this beautiful mnemonic for the spleen?

1, 3, 5, 7, 9, 11

One inch by three inches by five inches in size. Seven ounces in weight. Lies between the ninth and eleventh ribs.

Prohibition, Finnish, The end of

You will wonder how you got this far in life without knowing this.

543210

The exact time prohibition was lifted in Finland:
5th April, 1932, at 10am. The temperance movement was particularly active in Scandinavia and there was prohibition in Finland from 1919 to 1932. It is here solely on the grounds of neatness.

Body types

ENDomorphs have big **END**s

Mesomorphs are **M**uscular

Ec**T**omorphs are **T**hin

First Aid:

ABC – traditional method of checking what to do to treat a casualty.

Airways, Breathing, Circulation.

BBB – after an accident, what to check and in what order.

Breath Before Blood,

Blood Before Bones.

RICE – for sprains and bruises and sports injuries

Rest, Ice, Compression, Elevation.

When the face is red, raise the head;
When the face is pale, raise the tail.

Bulls and Bears

BUlls are BUyers

They are bullish, they are optimists. Prices are going to go up.

BUy. BUy. BUy.

BEars are sEllers

They are realists. Prices are going to go down.

sEll. sEll. sEll.

Firewood

A big old ash tree blew down in the wind in our garden recently, and a friend who was staying with us said it was the best wood to burn bar none. And he sent me a poem which made the same point:

Beech wood fires burn bright and clear

If the logs are kept a year;

Store your beech for Christmastide

With new-cut holly laid beside;

Chestnut's only good, they say,

If for years 'tis stored away;

Birch and fir wood burn too fast,

Blaze too bright and do not last;

Flames from larch will shoot up high,

Dangerously the sparks will fly;

But ash wood green and ash wood brown

Are fit for a Queen with a golden crown.

Oaken logs, if dry and old,

Keep away the winter's cold;

Poplar gives a bitter smoke,

Fills your eyes and makes you choke;

Elmwood burns like churchyard mould.

E'en the very flames are cold;

Hawthorn bakes the sweetest bread –

So it is in Ireland said;

Apple wood will scent the room,

Pear wood smells like flowers in bloom;

But ash wood wet and ash wood dry

A King may warm his slippers by.

So you can burn ash wood wet or dry, seasoned or not. It really is the best wood to burn. Sadly the ash tree is under threat from a deadly fungus, Chalara fraxinea, and may soon not be as common as it is at present.

The order of suits in bridge

Sue Hates Dealing Cards

Spades, Hearts, Diamonds, Clubs

Basic DIY

Which way to screw in a screw, or indeed, open a jar.

Righty tighty, leftie loosie

Basic Baking

For a sponge cake mix

(courtesy of my wife from her school days)

4, 4, 4, 4

4 oz self-raising flour

4 oz sugar

4 oz butter

4 oz eggs (2 eggs)

Basic flower arranging

You've been waiting for this one all your life, especially if you have a close friend called Colin.

Colin Tells Such Fat Lies:

This is for the elements of design in flower arranging:

Colour, Texture, Space, Form, Line

Flower arranging (cont)

Putting cut flowers in water:

The Harder the stem, the Hotter the water.

Deciduous/Coniferous trees

Deciduous trees Drop their leaves in autumn.

The others – Conifers – don't.

Deciduous can also describe ants that shed their wings after copulation.

Great Apes

Go Corgis

Gorillas, Chimpanzees, Orangutans, Gibbons.

Royal imperative for the Queen's favourite dogs.

Camels

Bactrian camel – two humps – capital B on its side

Dromedary – one hump – capital D on its side

Elephants

As Africa is much bigger than India, so African elephants are much bigger than Indian elephants. The ears of both are shaped like their respective continents.

India's big but Africa's bigger,

The same as their elephants

– it's easy to figure.

The novels of Jane Austen

JanE AustEn

His Lady PPS's NAME - PERson

The History of England

Lady Susan

Pride and Prejudice

Sense and Sensibility

Northanger Abbey

Mansfield Park

Emma

Persuasion

Sanditon

Chess

White is right

The colour of the square of each player's right-hand corner

Vitamins

A: 'Alibut, 'ake and 'addock. All fish in fact.

B: Brown Bread and Butter

C: Citrus fruit

D: Daylight

E: Easy – found in just about Every food.

Bee and wasp stings

Ammonia for a Bee sting – AB

Vinegar for a Wasp sting – VW

This is a long-standing mnemonic but there appears to be no evidence to show that vinegar is effective for wasp stings (although it seems to work with jellyfish stings).

The NHS Direct advice for a wasp sting is: wash the area, apply an ice pack, raise affected part, take anti-histamine if necessary.

All right – so does the famous Rugby Union Club London Wasps have a B team? They probably have, and they could still play in the same colours – yellow and black.

Winners of the Premiership

The English Premiership began in 1992 and is now, financially, the most successful football league in the world. Only five clubs have won the Premiership in its history.

Able Bodied Sea Man, Man

Arsenal (3), Blackburn Rovers (1), Chelsea (3), Manchester City (1) and Manchester United (lots of times, 12 at the last count).

Clunk click, every trip

The mnemonic slogan from a very successful series of public information films to remind people to wear a seat belt in the car. The seat belt was invented in Sweden in 1959 and introduced in Britain in 1965. It became compulsory for drivers and front seat passengers in 1983; seatbelts in the back of cars became compulsory in 1991.

The Government ran a high-profile advertising campaign in the early 1970s, and it is estimated that this humble road safety device has prevented 60,000 deaths and 670,000 serious injuries since 1983.

It was one of the safety moves, along with drink-driving laws, which has made Britain's roads just about the safest in the developed world. The death toll in 2010 was 1,857, the lowest since records began in 1926.

In 1966, the number of fatalities on the roads was 7,985.

The Seven Wonders of the Ancient World:

Peggi's Garb, Pal, Color, Temp

Def States Jo (Oz), To mahal

This is how mnemonics used to be. It will never be one of the wonders of the world and wins the prize for the clunkiest entry, but it does do its job, giving two clues for each wonder. If you can trust this to memory it certainly will come in useful one day.

1   Pyramids of Egypt (Giza)

2   Hanging Gardens of Babylon (Baghdad)

3   Pharos of Alexandria

4   Colossus of Rhodes

5   Temple of Diana (Ephesus)

6   Statue of Jupiter (Zeus) at Olympia

7   Tomb of Mausolus (Halicarnassu)

Or try PG: PC, DJ's TM

Parental Guidance: PC, the DJ's Trade Mark

Pyramids, Gardens, Pharos, Colossus, Diana, Jupiter, Tomb of Mausolus.

Snooker

You Go Brown By Potting Black

The sequence of the six colours after all the red balls have been potted

Yellow, Green, Brown, Blue, Pink, Black.

God Bless You

Snooker balls on the D from left to right:
Green, Brown, Yellow.

French

A useful way to remember the main verbs that are compounded with être in the perfect tense:

MMT Draper's Van

Monter, Mourir, Tomber. Descendre, Rester, Arriver, Partir, Entrer, Retourner, Sortir. Venir, Aller, Naître.

Latin

You may be asked at some stage the meaning of the beautiful Latin phrase, attributed to Thomas à Kempis (1418).

Sic transit gloria mundi

It does not mean Gloria was sick in the van on Monday.

The phrase is properly translated:

Thus passes the glory of the world

(Worldly things do not last for ever)

CHAPTER 19

Postscript

I once worked on a newspaper in the North of England and in the tape-room were two chaps whose names I always mixed up. It was embarrassing because I had dealings with them every day.

One was called Terry, who was always smartly dressed with a jacket and tie, and always, I remember, polished shoes. He became the Toff.

The other was called John. He was always casually dressed, with open-neck shirt and trainers – and he looked a bit dopey. He became the Jerk.

They couldn't have looked much more different if they had tried, but I'm sorry, the only way I could remember their names was to think of Toff – Terry and Jerk – John. Sorry Terry and John.

We moved house once and had to change the telephone number. The girl at the telephone exchange offered me a number of numbers to choose from, one of which was – well, the way she said it – 251 066. She offered me others, but then something clicked and I said I'll have 25 1066. The year 1066 – the Battle of Hastings – is one of the most famous and memorable dates in British history. Oh, that's a good number, she said, but because she was reading the numbers in groups of three, she hadn't seen it. Nor had other people, I suppose, because it was still available.

Think of the telephone number 891 011. Much easier to remember as 8 9 10 11.

It's not much, but it is an example of how you can sort and rearrange everyday data – it's useful in remembering PINs – to make life a little easier. One idea for remembering PINs is to use your favourite football team and remember the names of the players, and then their numbers.

On a completely prosaic note, it's easy enough and very useful to make up little mnemonics in your everyday life. Say I have four things to do – in no particular order – take a pill, write to the bank, email a friend (Robert), and ring school, I will make up something like this:

PSBR: This used to be, and maybe still is, the Public Sector Borrowing Requirement – take a Pill, ring School, write to the Bank, email Robert.

GBP: Great Britain Pounds: Don't forget to take a Pill, (a pattern is emerging here), phone the Garage and buy some Bread.

This book has been about ways of recalling bits of information that could come in useful sometime. If you are serious about increasing the power of your memory, there are a number of systems of varying complexity you can study. In days gone by, every literate person knew these memory methods; memory training was given the same importance as grammar and mathematics.

Tony Buzan, the British memory expert, identifies five different Peg Systems and has produced more than 100 books on the subject. You will have to work at them, but there is no doubt that you could improve your memory for some things in a very short time.

The oldest mnemonic system is the Loci or Place method dating from the 5th Century BC. Cicero attributed the system to Simonides of Ceos, who one day attended a banquet with a number of Greek luminaries in Thessaly. Simonides was called out of the room and as he stepped outside, the roof of the building collapsed. The poet closed his eyes and realized that he could remember where everyone in the hall was sitting. He identified who was sitting where, and therefore who survived and who was missing.

The system used loci (places) with which you are familiar, for example, your house. Think of some places or objects as you walk through the house – front door, front doorbell, entrance hall table, television, sofa, cooker, ring on cooker, sink, tap, etc. These have to be engrained into the memory, and then you attach the list to be remembered to it.

Say the list starts with milk, bread, coffee, and cereal. The story would start with a giant pint of milk by the front door and then a roll of bread acting as a doorbell. As you walked through the house, there would be a cup of aromatic coffee on the entrance hall table, and an advert for cornflakes on the TV when you went into the sitting room. And so on. Your home, however big or small, is a virtual 'memory palace'.

The Major System was invented in the mid-17th century, and developed the Peg System making it possible to remember very long numbers. Each number is allocated a letter, a consonant that has some connection to the number: The sounds can then be turned into words, which can become images. The key here is based on Harry Lorayne's book on super-memory published in 1958, which itself was based on earlier systems.

0 = Z/S	(sounds like zero)
1 = T/D	(one downstroke),
2 = N	(two downstrokes)
3 = M	(three downstrokes)
4 = R	(last letter of four)
5 = L	(Roman numeral for 50)
6 = J/SH/CH/G	(all soft, J reversed like 6)
7 = K/G /C	(all hard, capital K has 2 sevens)
8 = F/V/TH	(old-fashioned f resembled 8)
9 = B/P	(9 flipped makes p).

So 24 is NR, 25 NL, 26 NSH. Number 24 may turn into Nerd, 25 into Null and 26 into Ensure or (G)nasher. A bigger number might be 3482 MR (34) and FN (82) MRFN – Mr Finickity, a very awkward person.

Joshua Foer, a young American science journalist, had an assignment to report on the US Memory Championships in New York in 2005. He became interested in memory and befriended two young British 'Memory Athletes', who helped persuade him to enter the competition the following year.

His book, Moonwalking With Einstein, is the brilliant story of his odyssey, but more than that, an excellent introduction to memory and its extremes.

Memory competitions are a serious business, and Foer describes his training and the systems that he uses. He trained for at least one hour every day during the year and four and five hours in the last three months before the competition.

In the US final, there were a number of tests: names and faces, speed numbers, speed cards and remembering a poem. His tour de force was remembering a shuffled pack of cards in 1 minute and 40 seconds – 15 seconds quicker than the US record. He did this with just one year's training.

The reassuring thing for those of us who go upstairs and then can't think why we ever went there, is that a few days after Foer had won the US title, he went out to dinner, took the subway home and it was only when he got home that he realised that he driven his car to the dinner. 'I hadn't just forgotten where I parked it. I'd forgotten I had it."

There's hope for us all!

Bibliography

A Dictionary of Mnemonics, 1972
Baggore, RG: Historical Rhymes for the Young, 1909
Bellos, A: Alex's Adventures in Numberland, 2011
Benne, B: Waspleg and other Mnemonics, 1988
Blamires, H: Penguin Guide to Plain English, 2000
Buchan, J: As Easy as Pi, 2009
Buzan, T: Use Your Memory, 1989
Cook, V: Accomodating Brocolli in the Cemetary, 2004
Cunningham, S: The Story of Arithmetic, 1904
Dolby, K: Memory Magic, 2010
Dummett, M: Grammar and Style, 1993
Evans, H: Newsman's English, 1972
Evans, RL: Every Good Boy Deserves Fudge, 2007
Ewing Duncan, D: The Calendar, 1998
Ferraro, S: Remembrance of Things Fast, 1990
Flavell, L&R: Dictionary of Word Origins, 2004
Foer, J: Moonwalking with Einstein, 2011
Foley, E and Coates, B: Homework for Grown-ups, 2008
Fowler, HW and FG: The King's English, rep 1993
Gordon, K: The Transitive Vampire, 1984
Gowers, Sir E: The Complete Plain Words, 1970
Grey, R: Memoria Technica, 1732, 2nd ed
Harley 2341: mss British Library, early 15th century
Hartland, SJ: Big Elephants are Useful, 2008
Heffer, S: Strictly English, 2010
Hitchings, H: The Language Wars, 2011
Hughes, T: By Heart, 100 Poems to Remember, 1997
Lamb, BC: The Queen's English, 2010
Lorayne, H: A Super-Power Memory, 1963
Manser, MH: Secret Life of the English Language, 2007

Martin, S: I wish I knew that, 2010

Moore, J: Golden Ratio Geometry, 1996

Parkinson, J: i before e (except after c), 2007

Parkinson, J: Remember, Remember the 5th of November, 2008

Parkinson, J: Spilling the Beans on the Cat's Pyjamas, 2009

Partridge,E: Usage and Abusage – A Guide to Good English,1999

Phythian, BA: Foreign Expressions, 1982

Poskitt, K: Murderous Maths – Key to the Universe, 2009

Sampson, A (ed): I Wandered Lonely as a Cloud, 2009

Schott, B: Schott's Almanac, 2011

Sellers, L: The Simple Subs Book, 1968

Spence, JD: The Memory Palace of Matteo Ricci, 1984

Spiegel, F: Sick Notes, 1996

Stevens, C: Thirty Days has September, 2008

Stewart, I: Cabinet of Mathematical Curiosities, 2010

Stewart, I: Hoard of Mathematical Treasures, 2010

Struthers, J: Red Sky At Night, 2009

Taggart, C: An Apple a Day, 2009

Taggart, C: Guide to the Queen's English, 2010

Taggart, C: I Used to Know That, 2008

The Oxford Dictionary for Writers and Editors, 1981

Thomson, AJ & Martinet, AV: Practical English Grammar, 1990

Toseland, M; A Steroid Hit the Earth, 2008

Truss, L: Eats, Shoots & Leaves, 2003

Waring, C: I Used to Know That – Maths, 2010

Waterhouse, K: Waterhouse on Newspaper Style, 1989

Willers, M: The Bedside Book of Algebra, 2009

Acknowledgements

The entries in this book were collected over the last 40 years, during a life mainly spent in journalism. Many mnemonics are in the public domain, and I have created a number of new ones. I have tried to credit previous authors who have written on the subject and apologise if I have made any major omissions.

The book started, literally and figuratively, with the mnemonic The Siege of Sidney Street, the donor of which now lies in The Tomb of the Unknown Sub-Editor.

Two former Fleet Street colleagues have given advice and support throughout. Roger Sims was always available to help in any way, and Glyn Evans helped to sub-edit the copy. Many thanks also to George Jaworskyj for looking over the scientific chapters. Any errors are mine alone.

In the early days, staff at Gomer Press were very helpful, especially Pît Dafis and Gari Lloyd. Staff at the British Library, London, the National Library of Wales, Aberystwyth, and the Ceredigion Archives Office were both knowledgeable and patient.

I owe a debt of special thanks to Jenny Rosson, who

was very helpful and supportive from the start, and also thanks to Jim Anderson, Griff Bryan, Phil Bullen, Philip Chippindale, Dave Crowley, John Evans, Mair Harrison, Mike Heron, Sheila Middleton, Nick Sims, Emma Vaux, and Sarah Walden, who all helped the project in small and different but important ways.

Colleagues down the years have made small and probably unknowing contributions. I thank them all.

Readers will notice the complete absence of a discernible style to the illustrations in the book. This is not surprising as they are the work of a number of people. Michael Heath, the doyen of British cartoonists, did some drafts a while ago, which gave me a fillip when things were getting hard. I am eternally thankful to him. Ron McGeary was quick, uncomplaining and thoroughly professional. I also used the work of two art students, Rachel Hardwick and Sophie Thomas, and local artist Rhiannon Roberts, a recent graduate.

My elder daughter Hannah Bryan helped with illustrations and design work on this edition and I plead guilty to exploiting my ten-year-old daughter Ela. She did a good job, had the added advantage of being on the premises – and was cheap. Thanks to them all.

Finally, thanks to all at Llanina Books, and especially to my long-suffering wife, Bethan, for her patience.

NOTES

Publisher's Note

All readers whose contributions are included in future editions will receive a free inscribed copy of the new book, as well as an attribution.

Contact can be made at:
Llanina Books,
New Quay,
SA45 9SJ
www.llaninabooks.com
www.rogerbryan.com
roger@rogerbryan.com